CODE GIRLS

CODE GIRLS

THE TRUE STORY OF THE AMERICAN WOMEN
WHO SECRETLY BROKE CODES
IN WORLD WAR II

YOUNG READERS EDITION

LIZA MUNDY

Adapted by Laurie Calkhoven

Little, Brown and Company
New York Boston

Little, Brown and Company
Hachette Book Group
1290 Avenue of the Americas, New York, NY 10104
Visit us at LBYR.com

Originally published in hardcover and ebook
by Little, Brown and Company in October 2018
First Trade Paperback Edition: October 2019

Little, Brown and Company is a division of Hachette Book Group, Inc.
The Little, Brown name and logo are trademarks of Hachette Book Group, Inc.

The Library of Congress has cataloged the hardcover edition as follows:
Names: Mundy, Liza, 1960– author.
Title: Code girls : the true story of the American women who secretly broke codes in World War II / Liza Mundy.
Description: New York : Little, Brown and Company, [2018] | Includes bibliographical references and index. | Audience: Ages 8–12.
Identifiers: LCCN 2018023822| ISBN 9780316353731 (hardcover) |
ISBN 9780316353748 (ebook) | ISBN 9780316353755 (library edition ebook)
Subjects: LCSH: World War, 1939–1945—Cryptography—Juvenile literature. |
World War, 1939–1945—Participation, Female—Juvenile literature. |
Cryptographers—United States—History—20th century—Juvenile literature. |
Cryptography—United States—History—20th century—Juvenile literature.
Classification: LCC D810.C88 M862 2018 | DDC 940.54/867309252—dc23
LC record available at https://lccn.loc.gov/2018023822

ISBNs: 978-0-316-35377-9 (pbk.), 978-0-316-35374-8 (ebook)

Printed in the United States of America

LSC-C

10 9 8 7 6 5 4 3 2 1

To all these women,
and to Margaret Talbot

CONTENTS

FOREWORD

Dear Readers,

The young women featured in this book faced an incredibly difficult task at a time in American history when our freedom, our democracy, and our entire way of life were endangered, a time in global history when people around the world were suffering and uncertain of their fate. These women—not very much older than you are—had to learn hard, complicated work that many people thought they could not master. In many ways, these women had been treated for much of their life like children, their talents underestimated by the adults in their lives. When the young women accepted the job that was given to them, many people thought the responsibility and the challenge of code breaking might be too much for them.

Perhaps you, at some point in your life, have also felt underestimated—felt as though the adults in your life did not trust you or did not understand what you were capable of achieving. Perhaps you too have longed for the chance to prove yourself, to convince people you can do more than anyone realizes.

Well, this book is for you. As you will see, the women in this book proved that they could tackle most any task that was thrown at them. They stuck with the toughest challenges, mastering code systems that were intricate and ever-changing, in an atmosphere of great urgency, when lives were at stake and the work often seemed overwhelming. They pushed their brains and also their bodies, working around the clock. They emerged as leaders. They succeeded in cracking codes and doing tasks that people thought were impossible for anybody to succeed at, much less young women. If they failed one day at a certain message or code system, they got up the next morning and tried again. If they failed again that day, they got up the next morning and went right back to work. And again. And again. They understood that the fate of the free world really did rest on their shoulders. They withstood enormous pressure, they kept their work secret, and, importantly, they worked together. They supported one another. They believed in one another. They cheered one another on. They braved tragedy in their own lives, and they knew full well that the lives of men they knew and loved depended on their efforts. Imagine what that must have felt like—to know that your own brother's survival, for example, or the life of a good friend depended on you and your skills! They believed in America, and they believed in themselves. Even when other people doubted them, these young women knew they could do what was being asked of them. They gave it everything they had—and more. And they succeeded. At a critical moment in American history, they showed that when people are trusted with jobs of great difficulty and responsibility—even very young people—they can rise to the challenge and succeed. We all owe them our thanks.

I hope you find their tale inspiring, and I hope you find a challenge in your own life that you enjoy tackling and mastering. And don't let any doubters stop you! I am certain that whatever you want to take on, if you persist, you can do it.

Yours truly,
Liza Mundy

Codes and Ciphers

cipher: A secret message system in which a single letter or number is replaced by another single letter or number

code: A secret message system in which an entire word or phrase is replaced by another word, a series of letters, or a string of numbers known as a "code group"

cryptanalysis: The art and science of breaking codes and ciphers

cryptography: The art and science of making codes and ciphers

cryptology: Both making and breaking codes and ciphers

A World at War

During World War II, the United States and its allies (the Allied powers) fought against the Axis powers.

MAIN ALLIED POWERS:

France
Great Britain
Soviet Union
United States

MAIN AXIS POWERS:

Germany
Italy
Japan

The Secret Letters

December 7, 1941

The planes looked like distant pinpoints at first. No one took them seriously. An Army officer said the blips on the radar screens must be a group of American bombers arriving from California. A Navy commander, peering out his office window, saw a plane going into a dive and thought it was a reckless American pilot. "Get that fellow's number," he told his junior officer. "I want to report him." Then a dark shape fell out of the plane and whistled downward.

Just minutes before eight a.m., the planes burst into view. Nearly two hundred Japanese fighters and bombers filled the sky like a fast-moving thundercloud. Finally, the people looking at them understood.

Below the planes lay Pearl Harbor's Battleship Row, a

line of American warships. They were completely unprotected. Almost one hundred ships, more than half of the entire US Pacific Fleet, dotted the harbor. In nearby airfields, American planes sat wingtip to wingtip like fat targets.

One of the bombs found the USS *Arizona* and pierced the battleship's forward deck. It set off a store of gunpowder to create a giant fireball. The ship was hit over and over. It rose out of the water, cracked, and sank. Other bombs and torpedoes found the *California*, the *Oklahoma*, the *West Virginia*, the *Tennessee*, the *Nevada*, the *Maryland*, and the *Pennsylvania*.

A second wave of planes arrived an hour after the first. They dove, peeled off, and came back again and again. Ships and buildings were hit. Three battleships sank; another capsized. More than two thousand men were killed. Nearly half of the men who died were on the *Arizona*, including twenty-three pairs of brothers.

The American planes were destroyed.

News of the Pearl Harbor attack raced through the country. There were telephone calls and radio broadcasts. Newspapers printed special editions and people ran shouting along the street. Congress declared war on Japan the next day. Germany—Japan's ally—declared war on the United States three days later. Men flooded Army and

Navy recruiting stations in the weeks that followed. Every American felt affected by the tragedy.

War had been coming to America for more than a year. Even so, it was unthinkable that Japan would attack without warning. It was equally unthinkable that America's leaders had not seen Pearl Harbor coming.

These leaders knew that a failure on the scale of Pearl Harbor must not happen again. The country was fighting a global war against enemies who had been getting ready for years. Intelligence—the collection of information for military and political use—was more important than ever, yet extremely hard to come by. The Navy had a small, disorganized intelligence group. The Army had its own small operation. The United States had barely any spies abroad.

A first-rate code-breaking operation was necessary if America had any hope of winning the war.

And so the secret letters began going out.

Months before the attack on Pearl Harbor, the US Navy realized that it was way behind other countries in gathering intelligence. So a handful of letters appeared in college mailboxes as early as November 1941. Ann White, a senior at Wellesley College in Massachusetts, received hers on a fall afternoon.

She was invited to a private interview with Helen Dodson, a professor in Wellesley's Astronomy Department. Ann, a German major, was worried she might have to take an astronomy course in order to graduate. But she found that Helen Dodson had only two questions for her.

Did Ann White like crossword puzzles, and was she engaged to be married?

In all, more than twenty Wellesley seniors received secret invitations and gave the same replies. Yes, they liked crossword puzzles, and no, they were not engaged.

At Bryn Mawr, Mount Holyoke, Barnard, and Radcliffe, the letters went out to students from professors who were working with the Navy. The schools were founded to educate women at a time when most colleges would not admit them, when many people considered girls to be unworthy of higher education. But with men needed to fight, opinions changed.

Educated women were wanted. Urgently.

On many of these campuses, war felt particularly close. In the cold waters of the North Atlantic, German submarines preyed on US ships transporting food and supplies to England. In the terrible winter of 1942 students were rolling bandages, sewing blackout curtains, taking first aid courses, learning to do plane spotting, and sending bundles to Britain. Dorm rooms grew cold from lack of fuel.

The female students were called to secret meetings where they learned that the US Navy was inviting them to embark on a field called "cryptanalysis." That meant they would be analyzing and breaking the secret codes America's enemies used to communicate top secret information. The United States wanted to be able to read those messages. If the women passed a course in code breaking, they would go to Washington, DC, after graduation to take jobs with the Navy as civilians.

The women couldn't tell anybody what they were doing: not their friends, not their parents, not their roommates. They couldn't let news of their training leak, not even to brothers or boyfriends in the military. If asked, they could say they were studying communications.

And so the young women mastered methods of disguising letters and creating ciphers. They hid homework under desk blotters and strung quilts across their rooms so that roommates couldn't see what they were up to. Every week, their answers to a series of problem sets were sent to Washington.

The invitations spread beyond the Northeast to Goucher, a four-year women's college in Baltimore, Maryland. In a locked room at the top of Goucher Hall, an English professor and a Navy officer taught the secret course to the college's top senior girls.

One of the most well-liked students in the Goucher class of 1942 was Frances Steen. Fran was a biology major and the granddaughter of a shipping captain who ferried grain between the United States and his native Norway, which now was under Nazi occupation. Her father ran a grain warehouse at the Baltimore dock. Her brother, Egil, had graduated from the US Naval Academy. By the time Fran got her own secret letter, Egil's ship was in the North Atlantic. The Steen family was doing everything they could to support the war effort. Fran's mother was saving grease from bacon and giving away pots and pans to be made into tanks and guns.

Now there was something else the Steen family could contribute to the war effort: Fran.

As war engulfed the nation, the secret letters continued to go out. Code breaking was key to saving American lives.

At Vassar College in Poughkeepsie, New York, Edith Reynolds received a letter inviting her to appear in a room in the library. She stood, dazzled, with a few chosen classmates as a Navy captain covered in gold braid walked in. "Your country needs you, young ladies," he told them.

By that time, German U-boats had attacked shipping up and down the Atlantic coast. On the New Jersey shore, where Edith's family spent summers, bits of shipwreck washed up and they could hear guns booming. It did not seem out of the question that Japan and Germany would invade the United States.

The US Army, meanwhile, needed its own team of code breakers and set out to recruit smart young women. At first, the Army approached some of the same colleges the Navy did. Like the Navy, the Army wanted women who studied foreign languages as well as science and math. In the United States, in the 1940s, there was only one job available to a woman with such a fine education: schoolteacher.

And so—when the Navy objected that the Army was trying to steal "their" girls—the Army sent recruiters to teaching colleges. It was hard to find female students taking high-level math classes. Math was not a subject women were encouraged to study or to teach. In certain parts of the country there were no female math teachers at all. Those students who studied math because it was a passion jumped at the chance to serve their country in this way.

The Army needed more code breakers, and then more still. Going to teaching colleges wasn't enough. So it went looking for female schoolteachers interested in a new line of work. The Army sent handsome officers to small towns, remote cities, and farm communities, seeking women willing to move to Washington to serve the war effort, women who could "keep their lips zipped."

And so it was that on a Saturday in September 1943, a young schoolteacher named Dot Braden approached a pair of recruiters in the Virginian Hotel. Dot was twenty-three years old, dark-haired, adventurous, and confident. She was a 1942 graduate of Randolph-Macon Woman's College, where she studied French, Latin, and physics, and had spent one year teaching at a public high school. The eldest of four children, with two brothers serving in the Army, Dot needed to earn her own living and help support her mother.

Without knowing what she was applying for, Dot Braden filled out an application for a job with the War Department. A few weeks later, she found herself on a train headed to Washington, DC, with excitement in the pit of her stomach, very little money in her pocketbook, and not the faintest idea what she had been hired to do.

More than ten thousand women traveled to Washington, DC, to lend their minds to the war effort. The US military's decision to tap young women—and the women's willingness to accept the job—was a chief reason why America was able to build a code-breaking operation practically overnight. The fact that women were responsible for some of the most significant code-breaking triumphs of the war—and indeed, for shortening the war itself—was one of the best-kept secrets of the conflict.

The chain of events that led the Navy and the Army to recruit women is a long one. In September 1941, the US Navy asked Ada Comstock, the president of Radcliffe College, to identify a group of students to be trained in cryptanalysis.

The Navy was looking for bright women who had the ability to keep a secret, were born in the United States, were free of close ties with other nations, and had a flair for mathematics and languages. The Navy was also clear about the kind of women they did *not* want, including communists, pacifists, and anyone from a country or race being persecuted by the Germans, including Poles and Jews.

At the Navy's request, Comstock also approached leaders of other women's schools. Representatives from Barnard, Bryn Mawr, Vassar, Wellesley, Radcliffe, Smith, and Mount Holyoke met on October 31 and November 1, 1941. Ada Comstock handed out some materials the Navy had developed: a "Guide for Instructors" and an "Introduction to Students." The idea was that selected students would take the course during what was left of their senior year, then go to work for the Navy, in Washington, as civilians.

The wave of secret letters inviting young women to

secret meetings followed in the fall of 1941. Most of the women were in the top 10 percent of their class. The women were warned not to say the word "cryptanalysis" outside their classrooms. They were also told not to use the words "intelligence" or "security" to any person outside their study group, so as not to tip off the enemy.

In the late spring of 1942, the first wave of women recruited by the US Navy finished their secret courses and set out for Washington, DC, to start their duties. The women were told that just because they were female, that did not mean they would not be shot if they told anybody what they were doing. If they were asked what they did, they were to say they emptied trash cans and sharpened pencils. People believed them.

During the most violent global conflict that humanity has ever known—a war that cost more money, damaged more property, and took more lives than any war before or since—these women formed the backbone of one of the most successful intelligence efforts in history.

In the packets they opened before arriving in Washington, the women were told that, up to now, cryptanalytic work had been done by men.

"Whether women can take it over successfully," the Navy letter told them, "remains to be proved."

The letter added: "We believe you can do it."

Code breaking was a joint effort. The Americans had to cooperate with England's older and more sophisticated code-breaking operation, known as Bletchley Park. Thousands of Englishwomen had been hired to work there beginning in 1937, when it seemed as if there might be a second world war. The women operated "bombe" machines. These machines had been built to crack the Enigma ciphers used by the German Navy, Army, Air Force, and security services.

At the beginning, the Allies decided that the British would lead the code-breaking efforts in the war in Europe and the Atlantic. The Americans had the lead responsibility for code breaking in the Pacific.

As the war went on, the United States' code-breaking operation became central to the European conflict. More and more of the employees of both operations were women, as men shipped out to the hot, dry sands of North Africa, to Italian mountain ranges and snowy European forests, to the decks of Pacific aircraft carriers, to the beaches of Iwo Jima.

It was easy for the women's contribution to be overlooked. The women took their secrecy oath seriously. They weren't among the top brass and didn't write the histories afterward. And yet women were instrumental at every stage. They ran complex code-breaking machines. They built libraries and information sections. They worked as translators.

Women were often put in charge of "minor" systems—weather codes, for instance—that turned out to be key when major systems could not be read. And a number of mostly female teams broke major code systems.

It was a complicated position. Women were brought into the workforce to free up men for military service. As a result, men who had been doing office work were able to ship out to war. So women were welcome, but also resented. They themselves were trying to protect the men whose lives their arrival put in danger. They all had brothers, friends, and fiancés serving in the war.

In 1942, only about 4 percent of American women had completed four years of college. In part this was because women were denied admission to so many schools. Coeducational colleges capped the number of women they would admit. Families were more likely to pay a son's tuition than a daughter's. For a woman, a degree did not carry the same promise of future earnings that it did for a man, and many families did not consider it worthwhile for a daughter to attend college.

Those who did go to college were unusually motivated. Some came from families who valued learning for its own sake. Other families viewed college as a way for a woman to meet eligible college men at dances and mixers. Sometimes the women came from immigrant families— German, French, Italian—where having a daughter in college was a way of Americanizing the family as quickly as possible. Sometimes, a girl was so intellectually curious that there was no way to keep her away from college. It was not easy being a smart girl in the 1940s. People thought you were annoying.

What is interesting about this generation of women is that they did understand that at some point they might have to work for pay. Raised during the Great Depression, they knew they might have to support themselves no matter how "good" a marriage they did or did not make. And some women went to college because they planned to compete for the few spots in law or medical schools that were available to them.

In the 1940s, there were newspaper want ads that read "Male Help Wanted" and others that read "Female Help Wanted." For educated women, there was a tiny universe of jobs to be had, and these always paid less than men's jobs did. But it turned out that the very jobs women had been hired to do were often the ones that taught them the best skills for code-breaking work. Schoolteaching was perhaps the most important of these.

There were other women's jobs that turned out to be useful. Librarians were recruited to make sense of piled-up tangles of coded messages. Secretaries were good at filing and record keeping. Running office machines was a woman's occupation, and thousands were now needed to run the IBM machines. Musical talent is an indicator of code-breaking prowess, so all that piano practicing that girls did paid off. Telephone switchboard operators were not scared off by the most complex machines.

It was a rare moment in American history when educated women were not only wanted but competed for in the workforce. Up to now, many college leaders had hesitated to encourage women to major in math or science, because jobs for women in those fields were nearly impossible to get. Soon after Pearl Harbor, however, that changed. The men were gone but the jobs they left behind still had to be done. Female chemists, mathematicians, engineers, and designers were needed. The different branches of the military were competing with private companies and with one another to win their services.

This was seen as temporary. Sexism persisted: Educators worried that they might encourage women to pursue math and science only to see them left high and dry. One electrical company asked for twenty female engineers from Goucher, with the added request, "Select beautiful ones for we don't want them on our hands after the war."

The Axis powers didn't employ women the same way the Allies did. Japan and Germany were highly traditional cultures, and women were not asked to perform wartime military service. They rarely broke codes or did other high-level jobs, particularly in Japan.

The United States hired women by the thousands. On the eve of Pearl Harbor, the Army had 181 people working in a small, highly secret code-breaking office. By 1945 nearly 8,000 people would be working for the Army's massive code-breaking operation in Arlington, Virginia, with another 2,500 working in the field. Of the entire group, some 7,000—nearly 70 percent—were female.

Similarly, at the war's outset the US Navy had just a few hundred code breakers. By 1945 there were about 5,000 naval code breakers in Washington and about the same number serving overseas. At least 80 percent of the code breakers in Washington—some 4,000—were female.

Altogether, out of about 20,000 total American code breakers during the war, some 11,000 were women.

There are of course many reasons why the Allies succeeded in World War II, but the employment of women was one of these factors. It wasn't just that the women freed the men to fight. Women were active war agents. Through their brainwork, the women had an impact on the fighting.

———

After the war, the Joint Committee on the Investigation of the Pearl Harbor Attack noted that Army and Navy intelligence was "some of the finest intelligence available in our history" and that it "contributed enormously to the defeat of the enemy, greatly shortening the war, and saving many thousands of lives."

The fact that more than half of these code breakers were women was never mentioned.

World War I Code Breaking: A Matter of Life and Death

In its secret letters, the US Navy told its female recruits that they were embarking on work that had always been done by men. That was not completely true. Even before World War II there were some very important female pioneers in the world of cryptanalysis. Their breakthroughs became even more important after the war began.

Code breaking often makes advances during times of war, when it becomes a matter of life and death. But cryptanalysis was not a job that career military men wanted. And so wartime, exactly when code breaking was most needed, was exactly when women were invited to pinch-hit.

William and Elizebeth Friedman were a married couple with a fascination for code making and code breaking. After the United States entered World War I, William was sent to France to develop codes for frontline use, while Elizebeth oversaw a department that handled all the code and cipher work for the government in Washington.

When World War I ended, the Army hired both Friedmans, offering William a salary of $3,000 and Elizebeth a position at half that, $1,520. William worked for the Army for the next thirty years, while Elizebeth made headlines as a special agent for the Department of Justice in the 1930s working on smuggling and organized crime cases.

The US Navy, meanwhile, was developing its own female secret weapon as part of a code-breaking operation separate from the Army's. Agnes Meyer (later Agnes Meyer Driscoll), a brilliant young teacher who would become one of the greatest cryptanalysts of all time, enlisted in the naval reserves when the United States declared war on Germany in 1917. The Navy put the former math teacher to work encoding America's messages. She got her start making codes, which is the best possible training for learning how to break them.

Agnes would go on to train nearly all of the male naval code breakers who became famous for their World War II exploits.

CHAPTER ONE

The Most Difficult Problem

September 1940

The United States began beefing up its code-breaking operations months before the attack on Pearl Harbor. By September 1940, Germany had defeated Poland and Czechoslovakia. The Nazi war machine had overrun Norway and Denmark, defeated Belgium and so many others, and proceeded to march into Paris. Meanwhile, Japan was shouldering its way through China and around the Pacific. It was clear enough that sooner or later the United States would formally enter what was shaping up to be a second world war.

While the Navy tackled Japanese naval ciphers in offices nearby, the Army code breakers were attempting to penetrate one of the most complicated code systems they had ever come up against.

At the center of the Army's operation was William Friedman. Originally hired to develop codes for the US Army during World War I, Friedman had learned to break codes better than almost anybody in the world.

Friedman, now in his late forties, was a legend among the still-small global community of people involved in the making and breaking of codes and ciphers. In 1930 Friedman's bosses had given him funds to hire three young mathematicians: Frank Rowlett, a southerner who was teaching in Rocky Mount, Virginia, and Abraham Sinkov and Solomon Kullback, friends who had attended high school and City College of New York together. Along with John Hurt, a Virginian who could translate deciphered Japanese messages into English, the men had spent nearly a decade studying Friedman's methods of "attacking" codes and ciphers.

As the staff expanded, Friedman had begun hiring women. In the 1930s President Franklin Roosevelt's New Deal programs—programs designed to lift the country out of the Great Depression—had begun drawing women workers to Washington. Friedman also liked working with intelligent women, as evidenced by his own marriage to Elizebeth.

Elizebeth's example was even more valuable to her

husband than William Friedman knew. In October 1939, following the outbreak of war in Europe, the Army had given him the funds to enlarge his cryptanalytic staff. One of these early hires was Wilma Berryman, who had been attracted to the field thanks to Elizebeth's fame. Berryman had been trained to teach high school math. When she read in the Washington *Evening Star* about Elizebeth Friedman's exploits, she began to envision another future. She took a course in breaking codes and her answers made their way to William Friedman.

Berryman was hired and put on the Italian desk—which is to say, she was given a beginner's textbook on the Italian language and plunged into the secret communications of the government of Italy. That was how the Friedman operation worked. It was a teach-yourself kind of place. Newcomers would spend the morning studying training manuals and the afternoon attacking actual codes.

Wilma Berryman loved it.

So did Delia Ann Taylor, a tall, brainy midwesterner who graduated from Sweet Briar College in Virginia and had a master's degree from Smith College. Working near her was Mary Louise Prather. It was Prather's job to work the office machines that had been modified to assist with sorting enemy messages. Prather also filed the intercepted messages and kept a careful log of every last one.

And there was twenty-seven-year-old Genevieve Marie Grotjan, hired as a "junior cryptanalyst" in October 1939 for a salary of $2,000 per year (about $35,000 today). A native of Buffalo, New York, Grotjan had been a brilliant student. She aspired to teach college math but couldn't find a university math department willing to hire a woman. So she came to Washington and was hired by an obscure agency. When she took a math exam to earn a pay raise, her score attracted Friedman's attention. She received a call from the Signal Intelligence Service and was asked if she would like a job in the "code section." Grotjan didn't know what that meant, but she said yes.

After less than a year on the job, Grotjan was one of the team's most promising code breakers. Before long, she was assigned to the most pressing problem Friedman's office had undertaken: the cipher system used by Japanese diplomats around the world. It was a completely different system from that of their military counterparts. The Imperial Japanese Navy used laborious pen-and-paper systems. But Japanese diplomats favored newer machine-generated ciphers.

The small team that Grotjan belonged to was trying to do something that had never been done: reconstruct an unknown machine without having seen it or even a piece of it. They were attempting to penetrate the machine's inner workings by studying its output, sitting at tables looking at strings of random-seeming letters.

Inventors were always designing new machines to enable governments and businesses to keep their messages secure. Friedman was a master at finding the weaknesses of these machines. His employees often could break a "nut job's" systems in a matter of hours.

However, this new Japanese machine appeared to be unbreakable. It changed each letter of a message to a different letter, but nobody knew how it worked. No Westerner had laid eyes on it. The machine was not mobile like Enigma. It needed to be plugged in. Only the most important Japanese embassies were given access to it—those in Washington, Berlin, London, Paris, Moscow, Rome, Geneva, Brussels, Peking, and a few other major cities.

A machine-ciphering system worked well for diplomats. Phone calls were costly and could be listened in on. Tokyo often needed to send the same message to all its ambassadors, and rather than pick up a phone and make the same call, over and over, it was easier to hand a message to a clerk. The clerk would write it out in Romaji, a phonetic version of Japanese that used roman letters to spell out the syllables, as in *ma-ru*, for "merchant ship." The clerk would run "maru" through the machine, producing a new stream of letters—say, "biyo"—that could be cabled. The enciphering mechanism could be set in different positions, according to a key, or setting. The machine could be used in either enciphering or deciphering mode, so the diplomats could use their own machines to restore the message to its original meaning. They also could use it to write back to Tokyo.

The Japanese diplomats were discussing their country's war plans. They also were meeting with Hitler, the leader of Nazi Germany; Mussolini, the leader of Italy; and other key Axis leaders. If the Americans could uncover the machine's workings, they would have access to a priceless stream of information, involving not only Japanese intentions but those of every tyrant in Europe.

But first, they had to crack the uncrackable machine.

Army vs. Navy

It was not just on the football field that the Army and the Navy competed with each other. For several decades beginning with World War I, the two services built competitive and separate code-breaking operations. Each one wanted to be the best at breaking enemy codes.

When World War II broke out, both services needed to find intelligent women to help them fight the war. And they needed to find a way to work together and divide up the huge task in front of them.

The US Navy was primarily responsible for fighting the war at sea in both the Atlantic and Pacific Oceans. The Army fought on land in Europe and on the Pacific islands, along with the Marines.

The code-breaking units divided code-breaking operations along similar lines. US Navy code breakers tackled Japanese Navy codes and helped with the German Enigma messages. The US Army focused on Japanese diplomatic ciphers and the codes and ciphers of many enemy and neutral nations. But the Army's toughest assignment was breaking Japanese Army codes.

CHAPTER TWO

"I Have Something to Show You"

September 1940

Cracking the Japanese cipher machine seemed to be impossible. By the time that Genevieve Grotjan was assigned to the project, the Americans had been struggling for months. The first message in the new machine cipher had been intercepted in March 1939. The code breakers had known it was coming thanks to the fact that they had broken a simpler machine cipher that the Japanese used for much of the 1930s. The Americans called the first machine Red and the second machine Purple. Purple was more complicated than Red, which was why the code breakers were having such trouble with it.

The small number of Westerners who knew about the existence of the Purple cipher thought the Americans in William Friedman's tiny Japanese unit were wasting their time. The British had tried to break the Purple machine—as had the Germans—but both abandoned the job as undoable. The US Navy worked on Purple for four months but decided to concentrate on Japanese Navy codes. William Friedman's group was the only one that refused to give up.

After more than a year, the only thing the code breakers knew for sure was this: One weakness of the Japanese Purple machine stemmed from the fact that Tokyo had been too eager to save money. In the 1930s, when Japanese cryptographers were designing the Red machine, messages were transmitted in groups of four or five letters. Groups that could be pronounced were cheaper to send. To be pronounceable, a five-letter group had to contain at least two vowels. The Red machine therefore transformed vowels into vowels, and consonants into consonants, to ensure that "marus" (merchant ships) ended up as something like "biyav" and not, say, "xbvwq." That way, the messages remained pronounceable.

Friedman's team had figured out that the old Red machine employed two mechanisms to achieve this, one of which transformed the six vowels, the other the twenty consonants. They referred to these mechanisms as the "sixes" and the "twenties." The Friedman team had managed to build a facsimile of the Red machine. Their facsimile worked so well that Friedman's code breakers often were able to decipher a Red message and deliver it to US military intelligence before the Japanese code clerks had gotten the same message to their own bosses.

By the time the Purple machine came along, cable companies had relaxed the rule about groups needing to be pronounceable, so there was no need for sixes and twenties. Even so, new systems often contain elements of older ones. Banking on this, the code breakers hypothesized that the Purple machine also used two mechanisms, one that transformed six letters—any letters, not just vowels—and one that transformed twenty.

When the Purple intercepts started appearing, Friedman's code breakers were able to see that six letters appeared more often than others. But the Americans could not figure out how the remaining twenty letters were enciphered.

Genevieve Grotjan was one of the most patient team members. She would sit for hours contemplating streams of letters, making notations, creating charts.

William Friedman had taught his students that if you study a cipher long enough, from as many angles as possible, a pattern must declare itself. The goal of any code maker is to come up with a system that is random and therefore unbreakable. But this is a hard thing to do. Most machines used switches or rotors—set in new orders each day, according to the key or setting—to transform one letter into another, often several times. *A* might become *D*, and then *P*, and emerge as, say, *X*. The next time, the same letter would follow a whole new path. But wheels and rotors will eventually work through an entire cycle; at a certain point, they will come back to the beginning and encipher the same letter the same way. *A* will again become *D*, and then *P*, and then *X*. The more elaborate the machine—the more wheels involved, the more complex the settings—the longer it would take for the pattern to reveal itself. But at some point, something, somewhere, will repeat.

Friedman also understood that there are mathematical ways of detecting the underlying behavior of language and of individual letters. In English, *E* is the most frequent letter. If you are making a cipher and turn every *E* in a message into a *Z*, then *Z* will become the most frequent letter. One of the first things a cryptanalyst does is take a "frequency count" of all the letters in an enciphered message. If *Z* appears most frequently, this likely means *Z* stands for *E*. Ciphers quickly get much, much trickier, but it's remarkable what can be done with math.

What Friedman had also taught his team is that you can break a foreign cipher without understanding the language, as long as you know how the letters in that language behave. Certain letters, like *S*, often travel alongside certain other letters, like *T*, and he taught his staff to count how many times certain pairs—digraphs—appeared together, as well as trigraphs like *ing* or *ent* or *ive* or tetragraphs like *tion*. He knew on average how many vowels—between thirty-three and forty-seven—typically appear in one hundred letters of plain English. He knew which letters rarely appear side by side. He had even figured out how many blanks—or letters not occurring—tend to appear in one hundred letters. He had identified which consonants (*D, T, N, R, S*) are most frequent in ordinary English and which are least frequent (*J, K, Q, X, Z*). He studied how French letters behaved and how English behaved when sent over the telegraph. Since "the" is often omitted from a telegraphed message, the statistical behavior of *E* changes slightly in a telegram. These are the kinds of variations that code breakers live and breathe for.

Over a span of months, Friedman's code breakers had come up with every attack on Purple that they could think of. And yet they could not break it.

Friedman's team was under enormous pressure to break the Purple machine. When Purple first came online, they thought they could break it in a matter of months. As 1940 progressed and Jews in Europe were rounded up and the German war machine advanced, Roosevelt was anxious to know whether Japan would join in a formal alliance with Germany and Italy. Military intelligence visited Friedman every day asking whether he was doing everything he could. The code breakers urged radio intercept operators to ensure that the circuits carrying Purple messages were fully covered. They set up more IBM machines that had been modified to sort the Purple messages they were getting. And still: nothing.

Friedman liked his team to do their own pen work—copying out each letter. One technique was to write out the text of an enciphered message and print above or below it something they called a "crib." Cribbing is an essential component of code breaking—perhaps *the* essential component. Cribs are educated guesses about what the message says, or even what just a word or phrase probably consists of. Some minor Japanese ministries and embassies were still using the old Red machines, and sometimes Tokyo would send a message to all embassies using both Red and Purple. These were a great source of cribs. The code breakers could decipher the Red version and set it against the Purple cipher, hunting for connections.

The fact that they had broken the sixes meant they had

a few skeletal letters to work with to confirm the position of the crib, like in a game of hangman. It also helped that the US State Department was negotiating with Japan over a commercial treaty, so messages sometimes came through that contained quotes in English. The State Department would quietly slip the code breakers the originals, to use as cribs.

The code breakers formed a hypothesis about Purple, without quite being able to say why. They theorized that the Purple machine was using some kind of switching device to transform the letters. The design they hypothesized had four stepping switches. They thought there might be more than one set of four switches, using a cascading rhythm.

Buried in a stream of message text, it might be possible to spot letters that would show this. A code breaker might be able to detect a pattern showing the work of the switching devices. If this was true, there would be many letters between each repetition. But the repetition would exist. Somewhere. You needed a long message to find this; you needed more than one long message, really. And they had to have been sent on the same day, so as to have been enciphered by the same key.

Frank Rowlett and his Purple team looked for three

long messages sent on the same day and managed to find them. Now they needed a crib. Mary Louise Prather happened to recall a message transmitted on the same day in a lesser Japanese system they had broken. It was a marvelous feat of memory and gave them the crib they needed.

Frank Rowlett had work sheets made up with the same messages and cribs. He assigned the same sheets to different people, to see if anybody could find anything. They were sitting at tables scanning and studying.

It was September 20, 1940, at around two o'clock in the afternoon. Rowlett was talking with some of the other men when they looked up and saw that Genevieve Grotjan had materialized beside them. "Excuse me," she told them shyly. "I have something to show you."

She was "obviously excited," Rowlett recalled. "We could see from her attitude that she must have discovered something extraordinary."

Laying the work sheets on the table, Grotjan took her pencil and circled a place where two letters came together, one from the coded message, one from the crib. Then she went to a second work sheet and circled another coincidence, of two letters whose occurrence confirmed the very pattern they were looking for. Then, at the end of a long stream of letters, she circled a third. And a fourth. And she stood back. There it was. She had found the repetitions. She had confirmed the hypothesis. She had broken the twenties.

Many of the men Grotjan was working for had far more experience than she. They had written the textbooks she had studied from. Nobody quite understood how she'd done it, then or ever. Grotjan had a powerful ability to concentrate and, in that state of concentration, to see in a different way. In code breaking, counting and making charts and graphs and tables are part of the process. But when you have exhausted that, sometimes, in a deep moment of concentration, you see the thing you are looking for.

The men knew instantly what they were looking at. Grotjan had given them their entering wedge. While she stood quietly, they erupted in cheers. Frank Rowlett began yelling, "That's it! That's it! Gene has found what we were looking for!"

Genevieve Grotjan.

CHAPTER THREE

Magic

September 1940

Genevieve Grotjan's breakthrough was the victory the Army's code-breaking unit needed. The team could now construct a machine to decipher the Japanese diplomats' messages. Here is the thing about a machine cipher: It can be nearly impossible to break, but once you break it, you're in.

During the long ordeal, William Friedman had not been able to say anything to anybody outside the office, not even his wife. Even on the day of the breakthrough, he went home for dinner and said nothing. He couldn't. In the aftermath of the Purple breakthrough, William Friedman spent three months in Walter Reed General Hospital recovering from exhaustion.

Three years later, Friedman wrote a top secret memo

praising Genevieve Grotjan, Mary Louise Prather, and other members of the team in the highest possible terms. He described the Purple cipher as "by far the most difficult cryptanalytic problem successfully handled and solved by any signal intelligence organization in the world."

Never before, he pointed out, had a team of cryptanalysts managed to reconstruct a machine that nobody, apart from the enemy, had laid eyes on.

And here is the other thing: The Purple cipher didn't just give the Allies insight into Japanese thinking. As Friedman pointed out, the ability to read messages produced by the Purple machine provided "the most important source of strategically valuable, long-term intelligence" available to the Allies as World War II unfolded, including the thinking of fascist and collaborationist governments around all of Europe.

The team's breakthrough was held in the strictest secrecy. They would receive no public recognition. Only a handful of people could know the Purple cipher had been broken, because if the Japanese learned what had been accomplished they would stop using the machine.

The code breakers took a week to test their discovery. Friedman then shared their success with the small number of officials in military intelligence and Roosevelt's inner circle who were entitled to know about it. His private announcement was made on September 27, 1940, the day that Japan signed a pact with Germany and Italy.

Within two weeks the code breakers had built a copy of the Purple machine. Streams of messages were pouring in from Japanese diplomats in Berlin, Rome, Warsaw—all the key capitals of Europe. Often they were reporting back to Tokyo on conversations with Axis leaders. The messages were full of detail and often went on for pages.

For most of the war, it would be the Purple machine that gave the Allied nations their best information about what was being thought and said in Europe, especially Germany. This was largely thanks to General Baron Hiroshi Oshima, who served as Japan's ambassador to the Greater German Reich. Oshima enjoyed wide-ranging talks with Adolf Hitler. The Japanese ambassador admired the Nazis, toured German military facilities, and wrote reports back to Tokyo that were long, knowledgeable, and precise. Oshima's painstaking description of German fortifications along the French coast would be priceless later in the war when Allied commanders were planning the D-Day invasion.

All of the Purple dispatches were written by men who had their ears to the ground all over Europe. Going forward until the end of the war, the Japanese diplomats used the Purple machine to convey what Hitler was saying to his French collaborators; what people on the streets of Europe were feeling; what newspapers were writing; what Albert Speer, Nazi minister of armaments and war production, was reporting about munitions; what happened when a team of German officers tried to assassinate Hitler.

Early in 1941, several members of Friedman's team quietly boarded Britain's newest battleship, the HMS *King George V,* which had stopped in Annapolis to drop off the new British ambassador. They stowed one of their precious homemade Purple deciphering machines, hidden in a crate, on board, and—at great peril—took it across the sea, passing through the rattlesnake nest of lurking U-boats and presenting it to their amazed British colleagues.

Each day, messages were deciphered and a summary was typed on special paper with TOP SECRET printed at the top and bottom. The intelligence from the Purple machine came to be known as "Magic." The Magic summaries were put in a briefcase and taken by a messenger to the few people with the clearance to see them. In a 1944 memo, the Army noted that the Purple messages were "the most important and reliable source of information out of Europe." The sheer quantity was overwhelming to the translators who worked closely with the code breakers, converting the messages into English.

In April 1941, seven months after her historic break, Genevieve Grotjan received a raise of $300 per year and a promotion to "principal cryptographic clerk." Friedman's team rapidly began to expand.

———————————

The Purple machine could not predict the attack on Pearl Harbor, for the simple reason that Japanese diplomats were not clued in by their military as to what was about to happen.

At the time, there were 181 code breakers working in downtown DC for the Army. More began to pour in. Friedman's operation needed to relocate. The boom and expansion of the country's military administration had begun.

A group of Army officials noticed the spacious grounds and elegant buildings of a place called Arlington Hall Junior College. The school's location was convenient to Washington but far enough away to escape enemy bombing and the notice of secret agents. And so the War Department paid $650,000 for the property, and the faculty and 202 students were evicted. The move was so hasty that schoolgirls were still clearing out their rooms when convoys of vans secretly departed the Main Navy and Munitions Building, transporting machines and file cabinets stuffed full of intercepts.

Code breakers set up operations in the dormitory rooms, storing intercepts in bathtubs. Fences were erected, guard stations built.

The Purple machine was installed on the second floor but had to be draped with a cloth once every hour, when anybody who was not working on Purple was permitted to use the nearby bathroom.

At Arlington Hall, Genevieve Grotjan would stay on top of changes to Purple with a colleague, Mary Jo Dunning. The two women became familiar with the intricacies of the Japanese diplomatic cipher; it became like an old friend. As the war wore on, a number of other ciphers were attacked, and Grotjan would be assigned to solve them.

Arlington Hall soon found itself working the codes of some twenty-five nations. Some were codes; some were ciphers; some were both. There was a French code they called Jellyfish, a Chinese enciphered code they called Jabberwocky, another they called Gryphon. Some were important; some were merely interesting. Each week, top secret reports detailed breakthroughs, and it's striking how often they were made by women.

The tenor of the operation was changing. Top men like Sinkov, Rowlett, and Kullback received Army commissions and went into uniform. Military men took charge of some units, usually with a female civilian "assistant."

William Friedman was gently pushed aside: When he returned from convalescence he was given an office at Arlington Hall, working in an advisory capacity, but he no longer ran the place.

The majority of incoming workers remained civilians, following what had always been the hiring strategy in the Army's code-breaking unit. The hardy band of brothers and sisters from Friedman's original group retained their informal camaraderie, but they—including women like Wilma Berryman and Delia Taylor—would quickly find themselves in positions of enormous authority.

Sometimes, when she was riding the bus between her boardinghouse and the new Arlington offices, Genevieve Grotjan would look back on her moment of insight and remember it with "satisfaction and pleasure." Not often, though. She was too modest about her own contribution, and too busy.

The German Enigma Machine

The Germans used a complicated machine called Enigma to encipher their messages. The machine changed each letter of a word to another letter according to a setting. This setting for the Enigma machine changed every day, making the German messages especially hard to break.

Originally a tool for bankers, Enigma was invented by a German engineer in the 1920s. It was adapted for military use by the Nazis, and in 1933, Hitler ordered it taken off the market so his military could have sole access.

Enigma was a portable battery-powered device that could be lugged around and used during battle, or welded to the command center of a submarine. It had one job and one job only: to change each letter of a message to a different letter.

An Enigma operator inserted three rotors into the machine according to that day's setting. When a single letter was typed on a keyboard, the rotors would turn, transforming the letter over and over.

Each Enigma had more than three rotors to choose from, and each rotor could be set in twenty-six positions. There were millions of ways a letter could travel through the encipherment process.

The Germans believed Enigma could not be broken. They were wrong.

CHAPTER FOUR

"It Was Heart-Rending"

June 1942

The first six months of 1942, after the thunderbolt at Pearl Harbor, were a dark time for the United States, especially for the US Navy. At the outset of the war, the Japanese Navy had not lost a naval battle in more than fifty years. Japan had a brilliant top commander in Admiral Isoroku Yamamoto, who masterminded the Pearl Harbor attack.

Pearl Harbor was supposed to deliver a fatal blow to the United States. The attack didn't succeed on that level— US aircraft carriers were safely out of the harbor, and some battleships could be recovered and repaired.

But just hours after Pearl Harbor, the Japanese launched

air attacks on the Philippines. They captured Guam two days later and took Wake Island before Christmas. Meanwhile the Japanese Army was stabbing westward and southward. Hong Kong fell on Christmas Day 1941, Singapore two months later, Burma in May. The Japanese cut a merciless path through the Dutch East Indies, taking island after island along the Malay Peninsula—Celebes, Java, Sumatra, and Borneo.

February 1942 brought the worst blow to the American forces. After months of fighting, Roosevelt ordered General Douglas MacArthur to leave the Philippines. The US Navy's small cryptanalytic team there were smuggled out by submarine and taken to Australia. A small codebreaking unit remained in Australia for the rest of the war.

The attacks also devastated the British. "Over all this vast expanse of waters Japan was supreme, and we everywhere were weak and naked," British prime minister Winston Churchill wrote in his memoirs.

After Pearl Harbor brought America into the war, German admiral Karl Dönitz saw an opportunity: the unprotected Atlantic coast of the United States. The U-boat commander sent his submarines from Maine to Florida to sink freighters, tankers, trawlers, and barges. The goal was to destroy supplies produced to feed the Allied war effort.

Ships were sunk in full sight of horrified American citizens, who could stand on the beaches and watch freighters burning.

U-boats were invisible and noiseless. They would place themselves across the lanes used by convoys—groups of ships—and lie in wait. When a U-boat spotted a vessel, it would radio central command, which would alert other subs to close in.

England needed food. The Allies needed troops and war materiel to fight their campaigns in Italy and North Africa. Low-cost cargo ships—Liberty ships—were being produced in the United States in unheard-of numbers. But the U-boats in 1942 were able to sink ships faster than America could make them. Even worse was the fact that the Germans were reading the cipher the Allies used to direct their convoys.

The Allies also were reading the German Enigma cipher. A team of Polish cryptanalysts had in fact figured out the workings of the Enigma machine in the 1930s, and in 1938 they built six "bomby" machines that could detect possible daily settings.

In July 1939, before the Nazis overran their country, the Poles shared their discovery with the British and French. At Bletchley Park, England developed a method in which cryptanalysts could use a crib and write it beneath the cipher, then figure out, mathematically, what combination of settings might produce the cipher.

The British built sixty "bombe" machines, which, beginning in 1941, were run by some two thousand members of the Women's Royal Naval Service, or Wrens. The bombes would test a menu of settings to see if one could be a viable key setting. If the bombe got a "hit," then a message was fed into a smaller machine—an Enigma facsimile. If clear German emerged, the code breakers knew they had the correct key setting for the day.

The British at first kept their bombe project secret, even from their allies, for fear the enemy would find out and change the codes. Then in February 1942, the German Navy added a fourth rotor to the naval U-boat Enigma machines. The Allies called this new four-rotor cipher "Shark." It made it impossible to read U-boat ciphers. That was the beginning of an eight-month period of death and destruction. Ship after ship went down. It felt very much as though America and its allies would lose the war.

This was the atmosphere that the young women were entering when they graduated from college and made their way to the Navy offices in Washington, DC.

The Navy was still reeling from Pearl Harbor and the

Japanese victories that followed. America was losing the war on all sides and the atmosphere was chaotic. In January 1941, the naval code-breaking force consisted of just 60 people. By mid-1942 the number had increased to 720, with more arriving every day.

Up to that point, the Navy code-breaking office had employed some civilian women apart from Agnes Meyer Driscoll but treated them differently from men in terms of pay. Females were paid less than men doing the same job. Women college graduates who had taken an elementary course in cryptanalysis made $1,800 per year (about $27,000 in today's dollars); men with those qualifications made $2,000 (the equivalent of $3,000 more today). Women with master's degrees made $2,000, compared to $2,600 for men. Despite their unequal treatment by the Navy, the young women's arrival could not come soon enough. The Navy needed every single one of them to break codes.

In May 1942 Commander John Redman—head of the code-breaking operation—wrote each female student, begging her to get herself to the Navy building as fast as she could. "There is important work here waiting to be done," Redman told them. He gave each woman the address of the office and begged her to "keep me posted as to the approximate date of your arrival."

By now some students had become discouraged and dropped out of the program. Others married and moved to follow their husbands. Others did not answer enough problems correctly. And still more were rejected based on some aspect of their background. In all, 197 young women had received a secret invitation. Seventy-four found their way to DC, where they were employed as assistant cryptanalytic aides.

Goucher graduates Constance McCready and Joan Richter were among the first to arrive, showing up at the front desk on June 8, 1942. Viola Moore and Margaret Gilman, from Bryn Mawr, walked through the doors on the fifteenth. The rest trickled in toward the end of June and beginning of July.

The Navy didn't want to lose a single one. Fearful the women might quit if they couldn't find housing, the Navy wrote to each college president, seeking help in locating alumnae for the women to stay with. Women scrambled for rooms in basements, boardinghouses, and—in one case—the back half of the Francis Scott Key Book Shop in Georgetown, where a group of code-breaking women were allowed to borrow books and use the telephone in return for letting the bookstore staff use their toilet.

As quickly as they arrived, the women found themselves put to work. They were divvied up among the three shifts, known in the Navy as "watches." Fran Steen from Goucher and Ann White from Wellesley drew the midnight watch, from midnight to eight, while luckier souls drew the day watch, from eight to four, or evening watch, from four to midnight.

The summer of the Navy women's arrival was punishingly hot. The women would be dripping with sweat within half an hour of arriving at work. The Navy headquarters were crowded and unclean. Vi Moore, a French major from Bryn Mawr, was assigned the task of reporting how many cockroaches were crawling around in the women's bathroom.

The women's training had been rigorous. They had worked hard, but the problems they solved in their college courses were often very different from the actual work they were doing. And now they were responsible for men's lives. The responsibility felt awful and real.

Most of the women started out on the Japanese desk, but those few who knew German soon found themselves helping fight the Battle of the Atlantic. The British still had lead responsibility, but the Americans were doing what they could to help crack Shark, the new four-rotor Enigma cipher. Without the aid of bombe machines, the women used hand solutions to try to guess the day's key setting.

They were in constant communication with the British, trading notes and cribs.

Margaret Gilman, who knew some German, was put to work attacking Shark. In a small room guarded by Marines, Gilman and her colleagues labored over Nazi messages transmitted in the Bay of Biscay, the body of water off the coast of occupied France, where huge U-boat bases were located. Before the subs left base to attack Allied convoys, the Nazis would send out weather vessels to report back on conditions, using Enigma machines. There are a limited number of weather-related words—wind, rain, clouds—so it was sometimes possible to come up with cribs. "BISKAYAWETTER"—which means "Biscay weather"—was a crib the women often would try as they made charts and graphs of common cribs and the places in messages where Germans were most likely to place certain words.

The urgency of the work was stressful. "German submarines were literally controlling the Atlantic Ocean," Margaret Gilman recalled later. "Can you imagine sending out American troop ships loaded with soldiers through an Atlantic Ocean riddled with submarines? It was heart-rending, oh my God." In the unit's workroom, a detailed wall map displayed the Atlantic Ocean, with pins for every U-boat whose position they could locate. Margaret couldn't stand to look at the map. The morale of the whole country suffered when a troop ship was lost, and the women felt the burden of responsibility.

Ann White also was assigned to the Enigma unit, having majored in German at Wellesley. The work brought her into uncomfortable contact with the humanity of the enemy. The British were sending over items to help develop cribs. From time to time, they sent documents found in sinking or captured U-boats. These included things like family photos. Once, Ann's team broke a message from a Nazi commander announcing the birth of his son.

Mostly, the work was frustrating, and it filled the women with sadness and a sense of failure. Ann White's job was to translate German messages into English. During the winter of 1942–1943, her unit partially cracked a message alerting a group of German U-boats, known as a wolf pack, to a convoy of Allied ships passing the southern tip of Greenland. The code breakers, American and British, desperately tried to determine the location of the U-boats that lay in wait but could not. Later, they learned that most of the ships had been lost. "We worked on the Enigma desperately," Ann White would later say. "Blindly." It was a relief to be doing something: "Everyone we knew and loved was in this war. It was a godsend for a woman to be so busy she couldn't worry," she reflected. But "we knew men were dying."

The mood in the Japanese code rooms was equally grim, as women struggled to master the newest version of the Japanese fleet code. It was such an overwhelming effort that more than one commanding officer expressed the view that America might lose.

Japanese Fleet Codes

In the 1920s, Japan clearly wanted to build a Pacific fleet to rival America's. However, it lacked the natural resources, such as oil, iron, and rubber, it needed to become a world power. The United States knew Japan would look for those resources elsewhere in the Pacific region, threatening US territories. And so US Navy ships began intercepting Japanese messages.

In New York City, in 1923, naval intelligence officers secretly raided the office of the Japanese consul general, where they found a 1918 naval codebook, stole it, photographed each page, put the book back, and sent the pages to Washington. All of which ended up in the hands of the US Navy's Agnes Meyer Driscoll.

Agnes unlocked the secrets of the naval fleet code that Japan was refining during the 1920s and 1930s. She studied the stolen codebook day after day, year after year. She liked to say that "any man-made code could be broken by a woman."

Agnes figured out how the Japanese disguised their fleet code, using a method called "superencipherment" that involves both a code and a cipher. For the main fleet code, the Japanese were using a large codebook containing thousands of three-character code groups that stood for Japanese words, syllables, phrases, and even punctuation marks. Once a clerk wrote out a coded message, he then enciphered each character, somehow, so that the code group would be sent as a different set of characters entirely. The "research desk" knew what the code groups stood for, thanks to the theft of the codebook. But when they intercepted an actual message, the code groups had been enciphered. They had to figure out how to get rid of the encipherment and restore each code group to its original form.

The tiny Navy team worked for years to achieve this. It was Agnes Driscoll who realized that the encipherment was accomplished by switching the position of the characters.

Successful code breaking often comes down to the ability to see the whole rather than just the parts, to understand the system the enemy has created. The Japanese, Agnes diagnosed, were encoding their messages and then using something called columnar transposition, which involves writing the code groups out horizontally but transmitting them vertically, aided by a grid with certain spaces blacked out, whose design changed often.

Mastering the fleet code was a never-ending undertaking. As a security measure, the Japanese Navy periodically changed its codebooks—burning the old codebooks, printing new books, and distributing them to every ship, office, and island. When this happened, each word would be assigned a new code group, and the American code breakers would have to start from scratch. Sometimes, the changes were even bigger.

In 1931 the Japanese came up with code groups that were longer and organized in a tougher, more complex way. Puzzling out the new system took three years, and once again it was Driscoll who did most of the work in cracking one of the most complicated systems ever seen. It was the most difficult cryptanalytic task ever performed up to that date.

Then the Japanese code system changed again, and this change was even bigger. On June 1, 1939, the Japanese fleet began using a code that the Allies came to call JN-25. The Japanese—who had moved to using numbers rather than characters—now employed a massive codebook containing about thirty thousand five-digit groups. They also had a new way of enciphering. Before the code was sent, each code group was enciphered by using math to apply an "additive."

Here is how the additive method worked: When a Japanese cryptographer began encoding a single message, he would look in the codebook and find the five-digit group that stood for the word (or syllable or phrase or punctuation mark) he wanted. He would repeat that process until he got to the end of the message. Then he would get out a different book, called an additive book, turn to a page—selected at random—pick a five-digit number, and add that to the first code group. He would add the next additive to the second. And so on.

To make things even harder, the Japanese code makers used a peculiar kind of math called "false" addition. There was no carrying of digits, so 8 plus 7 would equal 5, rather than 15. If the code group for "maru" was 13563, and the additive was 24968, the resulting group would be 37421 (1 + 2 = 3; 3 + 4 = 7; 5 + 9 = 4; 6 + 6 = 2; 3 + 8 = 1). That was the group of digits that would be radioed. To crack a message, the Americans had to figure out the additive and subtract it to get the code group. Then they had to figure out what the code group stood for.

Once again, it was Agnes Driscoll who diagnosed the new system. Neither she nor anybody in the Navy operation had seen an additive cipher, but she figured it out. It took her less than a year to make a dent. She worked on it for several more months before being transferred in late 1940 to German systems—a promotion in the sense that the Atlantic Ocean was beginning to emerge as the hot spot in the early days of World War II. The research team continued working their way through JN-25, using her methods.

In December 1940, the Japanese Navy changed both the code and the cipher to a system the Allies called JN-25B. The team stripped the additives and built a partial bank of code words. Then, days before Pearl Harbor, the additive books were changed. The codebooks were not. The US Navy was able to recover a certain amount of the new system—but not enough—before the attack on Pearl Harbor.

If the Japanese Navy had changed both the codebook and the additives on December 1, 1941, there is no telling how badly the war in the Pacific would have gone. It was thanks in large part to Agnes Driscoll's decades-long detective work that America did not enter the Second World War quite as blind as it might have seemed.

CHAPTER FIVE

Midway

June 1942

In 1942, naval code breaking was laboring under a dark cloud. Pearl Harbor had called into question the value of cryptanalysis. Many top naval officials felt that code breaking took too long to be of use in the heat of an ongoing battle.

As the women streamed into the DC headquarters, male officers were sent to the Pacific to work on smaller teams set up near intercept stations. The field units could begin tackling messages as soon as they were plucked out of the air. These field teams sometimes deciphered more quickly, but Washington—with more machines and a bigger staff—would eventually produce more solutions. Often, though, Washington had to wait a long time for intercepts to arrive. Navy headquarters didn't have enough teletype lines. Some messages were sent by airplane, but many more were sent by boat and took weeks to make the journey. JN-25 was solved in agonizing bits and pieces.

Despite the Americans' frustrations in 1942, the Japanese were more vulnerable than it might have seemed. It was one thing to capture so many islands and bases, and another thing to supply and defend them. It was important that America's aircraft carriers had been safely out of harm's way during the attack on Pearl Harbor. World War II was the first war whose naval outcome would turn on aircraft carriers and the planes flying off their decks, rather than battleships.

Things had begun looking up for the code breakers just before the women's arrival in June. In early May, decoded JN-25 messages tipped off Admiral Chester Nimitz that a Japanese fleet aimed to capture Port Moresby in New Guinea. The Japanese were surprised when two carrier task forces of the American Navy materialized to meet them. The Battle of the Coral Sea, from May 4 to May 8, 1942, was the first naval battle in which the opposing ships never saw each other—the fighting was all done by aircraft—and it was the first Pacific contest where code breaking played a key role in the outcome. The result was a draw—the Americans lost the *Lexington*, and the *Yorktown* was badly damaged—but the Japanese losses, including many of its best-trained pilots, were bad.

By mid-May, the US Navy got wind of an even bigger Japanese operation. Thousands of messages began flashing back and forth in JN-25, suggesting that Japan was sending a massive flotilla somewhere. A lot of information was obtained about the planned Japanese operation, but there was one key puzzle piece that stumped everybody. In mid-May the Americans intercepted a message saying that the Japanese were headed to "AF." The code breakers could not be certain where AF was. The code-breaking team in Pearl Harbor felt sure AF stood for Midway, a tiny atoll where the United States maintained a base. Others thought the target might be Hawaii or the Aleutian Islands, off the mainland of Alaska.

So the code breakers hatched a plan. They instructed the men at the Midway base to radio a message in plain English saying that Midway was short on fresh water. The idea was that the Japanese would intercept the bulletin and pass it on. Just as they hoped, a local Japanese unit picked it up and sent its own message saying AF was short of water. The trick succeeded. AF stood for Midway.

Admiral Yamamoto's aim was to achieve the fatal blow that had eluded him at Pearl Harbor. He intended to send a small group to the Aleutian Islands as a decoy. US admiral Nimitz, he thought, would rush to counter that attack, but by that time, the rest of the Japanese fleet would be at Midway, prepared to finish him off.

But Nimitz let the Japanese head to the Aleutians and reinforced Midway instead. Thanks to cryptanalysts reading JN-25, Nimitz knew more about the planned attack than most Japanese officers did.

The Japanese showed up at Midway on June 4. They launched an air strike on the island, but this was no Pearl Harbor. American fighters met the incoming planes in midair, taking heavy fire but pushing the enemy back, while four waves of US bombers took off toward the Japanese carriers. The Japanese didn't know the Americans had aircraft carriers nearby. They soon would: From the decks of the *Hornet*, the *Yorktown*, and the *Enterprise*, torpedo and dive bombers took off.

The Japanese had expected a quick victory. By the time they called off the operation, the US Pacific Fleet had lost 2 ships, 145 aircraft, and 307 men. But the Japanese losses were devastating—4 aircraft carriers, almost 300 airplanes, and more than 2,500 men.

The four-day Battle of Midway was a huge American victory. It marked the end of Japan's expansion in the Pacific and was a major turning point in the war. The fact that an outnumbered American fleet had scored a win over an armada of enemy attackers lifted naval morale—not to mention the spirits of the whole country.

The Battle of Midway gave the Navy confidence in its cryptanalytic units and it gave the code breakers confidence in themselves.

Japan's ambassador to Nazi Germany, Hiroshi Oshima (left), was a confidant of Adolf Hitler (right). Oshima communicated with Tokyo using the "Purple" enciphering machine. Genevieve Grotjan's breakthrough enabled the United States to monitor Oshima's communications, yielding some of the best wartime intelligence out of Europe.

CHAPTER SIX

The Most Important Secret

June 1942

After Japan's shocking defeat at Midway, the Japanese decided to divide the fleet code into a number of "channels," so that certain regions or kinds of communications—Singapore, the Philippines, operational, administrative—had their own code and additive books. The volume of messages grew and grew. The naval code breakers received 18,000 JN-25 intercepts per month in the first six months of 1942, and more than double that, 37,000, in the second half of the year. By the fourth quarter of 1943 they would be getting 126,000 messages per month.

This was the time when most of the women were assigned to JN-25. They had no idea what they were getting into, but they were delighted to be there. The task was so large that the women instantly took on real responsibility.

The women rose to the challenge. Anne Barus, a Smith history major, was assigned to recover additives, a task her training course had not covered. It involved mental math performed day after day, week after week, for more than three years. The women in her unit were given big sheets of paper, about a yard long and two feet wide. Each sheet was filled with rows of five-digit numbers—14579 35981 56921 78632 90214, say—that also lined up in vertical columns. It was Anne's job to figure out what the additives were, so that the Japanese additive book might be reconstructed.

To do this, Anne had to master the same "false math" the Japanese used—only in reverse. She and her colleagues had to start with the enciphered numbers and work backward to find the underlying code group. And they had to do it fast. Looking down a vertical column, Anne had to find the additive used to encipher all the code groups in that column.

Aside from her own wits, Anne had one thing to help her: a quirky feature designed to cope with the fact that radio signals were sometimes distorted and hard to hear. This garble was a huge problem in radio transmissions, so the Japanese developed clever "garble checks" so the person at the receiving end could do a bit of math to be sure the message had transmitted correctly. Many of these checks helped with breaking the messages.

One garble check was the rule that a code group was always divisible by three. Looking at her work sheet, Anne would guess a possible additive, then go down the vertical column, quickly, in her head, stripping the additive out of each group she saw, and looking to see if the remainder was divisible by three. If she guessed an additive, stripped it, looked at the row of code groups, and saw that all were divisible by three—17436, say, or 23823—then she knew she had gotten down to valid code groups. It took all this work to get one single additive, which would be recorded in the book they were building. Whenever the Japanese changed the JN-25 cipher books, the unit would start all over again. It was like sweeping the sand from a beach.

Anne, like the other women in her room, learned to look for common enemy mistakes. Sometimes a radioman would send a message in plain Japanese that others were sending in code. The women could use the plain Japanese as a crib. Japanese merchant ship captains often sent a *shoo-goichi* message, stating what their exact position would be at noon. Anne learned the code groups for "noon position," and she learned where the phrase was likely to appear. When she saw an enciphered group in that place, she could subtract the code group and obtain the additive.

Sometimes, enemy cryptographers liked to begin a message in the middle. When they did this, they would include a code group that stood for "begin message here" to show where the message started. The women learned the code groups for "begin message here"—there were several—and gained another point of entry.

Whenever the women saw a mistake, they pounced. The *shoo-goichi* messages not only helped recover additives. The noon position would be radioed to an American submarine captain, who would be waiting for the Japanese ship when it appeared on the horizon.

It was boring, tedious work, except when it wasn't. As the number of messages increased, the number of women in the ranks of people solving them grew. By the fourth quarter of 1943, 183 men and 473 women were working on JN-25 in Washington—more than twice as many women as men. One memo noted that it was impossible to keep the women in the dark as to what the messages said. The most important secret was the fact that JN-25 was being worked at all.

The women kept that secret. They were outraged when the truth about Midway's success made its way into the press. On June 7, 1942—while the battle was still going on—the *Chicago Tribune* published a blockbuster story in its Sunday edition, headed: JAP FLEET SMASHED BY U.S. 2

CARRIERS SUNK AT MIDWAY: NAVY HAD WORD OF JAP PLAN TO STRIKE AT SEA; KNEW DUTCH HARBOR WAS A FEINT. The article noted that the makeup of the Japanese forces "was well known in American naval circles several days before the battle began." The news was hushed up by the Office of Censorship out of fear that the Japanese would take note, but it may have been too late.

The Japanese made another major overhaul of JN-25 not long after, and many code breakers were convinced this new changeover was a reaction to the news getting out.

The Japanese changed JN-25 just as the US Navy began to succeed in the Pacific. Fortunately the US Navy had made the wise decision to set up a smaller unit to tackle what were called "minor ciphers." In the vast Pacific Ocean, not every message could travel in the main fleet code. The Japanese used secondary systems to communicate between captured islands, between weather lookouts and rice ships, or even just to broadcast water levels and fishing conditions. They also devised temporary "contact codes" for use in battle.

The minor-cipher unit was under the charge of Frank Raven, a Yale graduate and brilliant cryptanalyst. His team was working "Japanese miscellaneous," plucking intercepts out of random piles in the Navy building that were accumulating in a junk box marked "W." The crew broke at least one system per week beginning in March 1942, and now women were replacing men on that crew. Among these were Bea Norton and Bets Colby, both members of the first group of Wellesley graduates to go to Washington. The unit's main ongoing task was deciphering an "inter-island cipher," which was known in official documents as JN-20.

During the many times when the big fleet code went dark—meaning the JN-25 books changed and the code breakers could not read the code—the island cipher proved a rich source of intelligence.

For the women working in Raven's unit, the inter-island ciphers gave vivid glimpses of the warfare unfolding on volcanic beaches and in thick island jungles thousands of miles away. When US Marines hit the beaches of Guadalcanal in August 1942, Raven's crew began to work a cipher set up by the Japanese as an emergency form of communication between the Japanese on the island and the fleet at sea. As the US Marines pursued them, a small band of Japanese retreated into the jungle, sending twenty or thirty messages a day in the tiny makeshift cipher. It gave the women a sad image of what it felt like to face certain death. "I have not seen the sea for two weeks," said one message. "I have not seen the sky for three weeks. It is time for me to die for the Emperor." The number of Japanese resisters dwindled until, as Raven put it, the "three or four men who were left got into a motor-boat; we followed them daily in JN-20 as they described the bad conditions, etc. We sank the boat."

"I felt so lucky to be in this small interesting unit," said Bea Norton later, "and to feel my work had some value." The work was difficult, but thrilling at the same time. The women knew they were making a real difference in the war. "Never in my life since have I felt as challenged as during that period," reflected Ann White.

They were doing such valuable work that Donald Menzel—a Harvard astronomy professor who was the point person for Navy recruiting at Harvard and Radcliffe—wrote Ada Comstock about the good things he was hearing from their bosses. "The women are arriving in great numbers and...they are proving very successful. Those who have written me are delighted with the work and find it interesting and exciting beyond all expectation."

Preparations were made for the next group of female trainees. Of the 247 seniors in the class of 1943 who took the course, 222 finished and made their way to Washington. Even with these new arrivals, the Navy began to see that ever more women would be needed to get the job done.

The WAVES Anthem

In July 1942, Roosevelt signed the law creating a women's naval reserve. They were called WAVES—Women Accepted for Volunteer Emergency Service. They marched to chapel on Sundays, where they were joined by men doing officer training. The WAVES had a song written as a counterpoint to "Anchors Aweigh":

> *WAVES of the Navy,*
> *There's a ship sailing down the bay.*
> *And she won't slip into port again*
> *Until that Victory Day.*
> *Carry on for that gallant ship*
> *And for every hero brave*
> *Who will find ashore,*
> *his man-sized chore*
> *Was done by a Navy WAVE.*

During services the men would sing the original and the women would counter with their lyrics. The harmony was so moving and powerful that Frances Lynd, from Bryn Mawr's class of 1943, said it made the hair stand up on the back of her neck.

CHAPTER SEVEN

WAVES

July 1942

Women were proving so useful to the war effort that a new field opened to them: military service. By 1942 England and Canada had admitted women into their military. Still, the idea of putting American women into military uniform was controversial.

"Who will then do the cooking, the washing, the mending, the humble homey tasks to which every woman has devoted herself; who will nurture the children?" thundered one congressman.

Before the war, men and women in the United States had what were seen as "traditional" roles. Men went out to work, and women stayed home to take care of the children and the house. If women joined the military, some people wondered, would they become too much like men? Would men want to marry women who had been in the military?

But America was fighting a two-ocean war. American men alone were not enough. The military needed women to win.

US Army leaders liked the idea of having women doing clerical and encoding work. President Roosevelt signed the Women's Army Auxiliary Corps (WAAC) bill into law in May 1942. Women were allowed into the Army on an "auxiliary," or inferior, basis. WAACs were paid less than men and did not hold the same ranks or receive the same benefits. The word "auxiliary" was dropped in 1943 and the WAACs became WACs, but women were still not treated as equals.

Even so, women fell over themselves to enlist. 10,000 WOMEN IN U.S. RUSH TO JOIN NEW ARMY CORPS, wrote the *New York Times* on May 28, 1942. The Army women could not serve in combat, but they served as drivers, accountants, draftsmen, cooks, occupational therapists, and encoders. Despite fears that women would become hysterical in emergencies or that female voices were too soft to be heard, WACs worked in airplane control towers and did well.

In May 1942, President Roosevelt urged the Navy to get a move on and admit women. So did First Lady Eleanor Roosevelt. It was an uphill battle, but one that they won. In July 1942, Roosevelt signed the law creating a women's naval reserve. They were called WAVES—Women Accepted for Volunteer Emergency Service.

The number of women who rushed to join shocked even Elizabeth Reynard, an English professor from Barnard who was appointed special assistant to the chief of naval personnel, Admiral Randall Jacobs. She received from Jacobs what would become a famous telegram: "Women off the port and starboard bows. Visibility zero. Come at once."

The Navy women were not an "auxiliary" like the women in the WAACs, but a naval reserve like the men's. But there were still inequalities. Women reservists were entitled to the same pay as men, but not to retirement benefits. At first they could not hold top ranks, and the female director of the WAVES was often cut out of important decisions.

There were many arguments about the women's uniforms. Josephine Ogden Forrestal, whose husband, James Forrestal, would soon become secretary of the Navy, approached the fashion house Mainbocher. The end result was spectacular.

The WAVES uniform consisted of a navy blue wool jacket, a flattering skirt, a white short-sleeved shirt, a tie, and an elegant dusty blue braid. The uniform was topped by a dashing little hat and a square black pocketbook that strapped diagonally over the shoulders. The women were also issued raincoats with roomy hoods and were expected to wear white or black gloves. No jewelry could be worn and umbrellas could not be carried. The WAVES were expected to be in uniform at all times, except when wearing athletic clothing or being court-martialed.

The uniform conveyed to the public that the Navy cared about its women. A number of code breakers admitted that the Mainbocher uniform was one reason they enlisted. Some felt it was the most flattering clothing they ever owned. Others chose the Navy over the Army because they preferred the classic Navy blue over the drab khaki that was the fate of the WACs. The Army women even had to wear khaki underwear, which the WAVES thought was hilarious. Navy women felt superior in being able to wear their own underwear.

Women working as civilian code breakers in Washington could now be commissioned as officers in the US Navy Reserve. They were given a choice. Some stayed on as civilians, but the majority accepted commissions. Officer status would give them more authority with their male counterparts, and in many cases it came along with a pay raise.

And so, in the fall and winter of 1942, just as the women were truly settling into their new jobs, they had to leave the DC headquarters for officer training camp. The men were reluctant to let them go. JN-25 had gone dark again. The U-boat Enigma cipher was likewise unreadable. It was a grim time. The Navy decided to stagger the women's departure. Six were sent to officer training in October, another handful in November, and so on.

A WAVES officer training school was established at Smith College in Massachusetts, and another at Mount Holyoke. In late 1942, Bea Norton, Fran Steen, Ann White, Margaret Gilman, Vi Moore, and the rest were sent north. The number of women on the Smith campus doubled overnight.

The women didn't have uniforms yet, and so they drilled in civilian clothes, wearing black Oxford shoes with one-and-a-half-inch heels. The heels presented a problem. When they were marching and had to back up, the women sometimes fell backward on their rears. During classroom time, they received standard naval instruction. They learned all the Navy lingo. A work shift was a "watch." You were "welcomed aboard" when you joined your unit. The thing you walked on was a "deck," not a floor, even if it was in a building. Personal possessions were "gear." To assemble was to "muster." A meal was a "mess." If you were out sick you were "on the binnacle list." The bathroom was, of course, "the head."

The women learned the lines of a battleship, the functions of a destroyer, and how many guns were on a cruiser. They were taught to recognize the silhouettes of enemy ships and airplanes, a skill they would never need. WAVES were not permitted overseas. Even so, they had to get the same vaccinations men did: shots for diphtheria, smallpox, typhoid, and tetanus, administered by means of a "daisy chain," a system in which the women walked forward as they were jabbed with needles from both sides.

The women agreed to serve for the duration of the war plus six months. Reveille was at five thirty a.m. and lights were out by ten p.m. The women had to make up their beds shipshape and seamanlike. That meant square corners and the blanket folded in half, then in thirds, then in half again, placed at the bottom of the bed. The cover had to be so tight a quarter would bounce on it. The woman on the top bunk was required to sleep with her head at the opposite end from the woman on the bottom. Shoes had to be lined up in the closet with toes facing out.

They had to do the same calisthenics men did. If a woman couldn't shinny up a rope, others helped. One unit included a woman named Lib who was working on a top secret joint project between the Navy and private industry.

Lib couldn't shinny to save her life, and all the women, knowing how important Lib's brain was to the war effort, tried their best to hoist her upward.

They no longer existed as individuals. Everyone's hair had to be above her collar. If your hair was too long, your roommate cut it. The women bunked four to a room. They had to identify themselves as "seamen" when addressing an officer. They also learned how to salute. The first WAVES officers at Smith were reviewed by Eleanor Roosevelt. Ordered to salute the first lady, they put their hands up but let their thumbs drift and ended up thumbing their noses at Mrs. Roosevelt. Later classes were warned not to make the same mistake. They were told, when saluting, to tuck their thumbs firmly against their forefingers.

The women were warned that everything they did would reflect on the WAVES. "As you no doubt have discovered, where a WAVE goes, all eyes go," they were instructed in a newsletter, which told them that a self-respecting member of the WAVES does not "slouch over desks and counters when she talks to others; she maintains a neat, clean, well-pressed appearance at all times; she wears her hat straight...and does not wear flowers at any time on any part of her uniform."

And they marched. Everywhere. The women would

go out in the gray dawn and make formation. They marched on the street, on the campus, on the playing fields. If a woman fell or fainted—woman overboard—they were told to step around her and leave her lying where she fell. While they marched, they sang. They sang sea chants, and they sang songs that had been written or changed for the WAVES, often based on popular tunes. The songs included lyrics such as:

> *I don't need a man to give me sympathy*
> *Why I needed it before is a mystery*

And:

> *Honor a glorious past*
> *Strive for a future bright*
> *For, like our men at sea*
> *We, too, will fight*

The women loved every part of it. They took meals at Wiggins Tavern, which they loved. They loved the marching and parades. They loved having a purpose in the war. The Navy used extra drills as a punishment, but that didn't work with the women. They liked the marching too much to feel they were being punished. They sang and sang. They felt love for the men they were replacing.

People came from everywhere to take pictures of a WAVES officers' graduation. When the women graduated, they received their uniforms, with bars to show they were ensigns. They felt that they belonged to the US Navy.

The women code breakers were not allowed to stay in officer training long. Most were snatched away after only four weeks and brought back to Washington, DC. The night before departing, they lined up to receive their uniforms.

In Washington, nobody had seen a woman in military uniform. The women stopped traffic. Cars had fender benders. At the Navy itself, the first group got a mixed reception. Their bosses were glad to see them, but Bea Norton felt the Marines guarding each room took pleasure in making the women salute over and over. Blanche DePuy sensed resentment that women were in uniform alongside men. Her father was a colonel in the Army, so she was used to military nonsense. Nancy Dobson from Wellesley was asked by a male officer to sew on a button—a task every Navy man knows how to do for himself—and was scolded when she sewed it upside down.

But other women enjoyed their new status. In her office in the Japanese unit, Fran Steen found that even as

an ensign—the lowest officer rank—she was the top officer. There was nobody who outranked her. Her hair was
slightly longer than it should have been, but there was
nobody to order her to cut it. The men were being shipped
out that fast, and the women code breakers were coming in.

A recruiting poster aimed at drawing women into Navy service.

CHAPTER EIGHT

Uncle Sam Wants You!

July 1942

Now that the WAVES had been created, any and all women who met recruiting qualifications could sign up. There was no need for a secret letter. Mail trucks were emblazoned with a poster saying that Uncle Sam wanted women to join the US Navy.

The US Navy's basic requirements for female officers were a college degree or two years of college plus two years of work. Regular enlisted women, meaning non-officers, could get by with a high school degree. More women than expected answered the call. Officials thought there might be ten thousand WAVES. More than one hundred thousand women would serve by the time the war was over.

Women joined up for all sorts of reasons—because they

were patriotic and wanted to help win the war; because they didn't have any brothers and wanted to represent their family in the war effort; because they did have brothers and wanted to bring them home. At the outset there was a cap limiting the number of officers, so many overqualified college women enlisted as ordinary seamen, just to get in.

Depending on their qualifications, the WAVES were funneled into officer or enlisted training. Recruits underwent physical exams along with aptitude and intelligence tests as well as interviews and vocational exams. Then they were sent on for specialized training. A WAVES enlistee might end up rigging parachutes, training carrier pigeons, working as a "weather girl," operating a radio receiver, or learning the standard yeoman's duties of clerking and bookkeeping. But more than three thousand enlisted women who tested high for intelligence and loyalty as well as secretarial skills would be quietly informed that they were headed to communications training and then on to Washington, DC. They had been selected as code breakers.

Troop trains carried women across the country. Women from rural areas were amazed to ride through cities where people pulled clotheslines back and forth between apartment buildings. Georgia O'Connor joined the WAVES out of curiosity, attracted by the smart uniforms, the hope of adventure, and the desire to see whether she could pass the tests. Ava Caudle joined because she had grown up on a North Carolina farm so remote that the most exciting event of the month was the arrival of the bookmobile. As a girl, she had never seen a movie. These women were selected to work in the code-breaking operation. Many would find themselves doing the same work the college-educated women were.

Myrtle Otto enlisted even before her own brothers did. En route to Cedar Falls, Iowa, where a basic-training camp was established at Iowa State Teachers College, she got on a train that left Boston's South Station and traveled north to Canada; down through Kalamazoo, Michigan; to Chicago; across the Mississippi; and on to Iowa. It was the first time she'd ridden in a sleeper car. At Cedar Falls, the women were issued uniforms. Enlisted Navy women had to wear heavy lisle stockings that made their legs look as thick as logs. They took showers by numbers, one girl at the first bell, another one at the next, with three minutes to dress after you showered. It got so cold in Cedar Falls that when the women would put bottles of Coke on the windowsill to chill, the liquid would freeze overnight and pop the bottle top off, and the Coke would expand upward and freeze like a fountain.

A number of the WAVES selected as code breakers met resistance from their families when they enlisted.

Ida Mae Olson was born in Colorado and attended a tiny country school where she was the only student in the fifth grade. She was working as a nurse's aide in Denver when her roommate enlisted. She couldn't afford the rent on her own, so she enlisted too. Her mother objected that "only bad women join the service. You know, wild women." Ida Mae joined up anyway, and her mother came around. "When I would come home on leave, she'd take pictures of me in uniform. She'd be so proud."

Some mothers were unhappy that their sons were being sent into combat thanks to the women coming in to take over their desk jobs. But others thought the WAVES were wonderful and would invite them home for milk and cookies or holiday meals.

Basic training was a learning experience in more ways than one. On the train to Cedar Falls, Betty Hyatt, who up to then had never left rural South Carolina, wondered aloud "what a Jewish girl looks like." She learned to her mortification that the girl beside her, angry and offended, was Jewish. She hastily apologized. Up to that point she had never met anybody who was Jewish or Catholic. At Cedar Falls, the tables were turned and she took grief for being southern. Since northerners sometimes believed southern-ers to be slow, her teacher remarked upon how odd it was that Betty was the fastest typist in the class. She flunked the swim test, but—having taken the IQ test—was told she was being given special permission and sent to Washington. When she asked if she had passed the intelligence test, the commander replied: "Did you ever."

The women officers continued to train at Smith and Mount Holyoke, but by February 1943, boot camps for enlisted WAVES were combined on the campus of Hunter College in the Bronx, New York, which could hold five thousand women at a time. Some ninety thousand women went through six weeks of basic training at the USS Hunter. Residents of nearby apartments were evicted to house them. The Navy now saw how valuable these women were.

The women began working as gunnery instructors, storekeepers, pharmacists' mates, and instructors showing male pilots how to use the flight simulators. The codebreaking unit had to compete to get them.

For the women, coming to New York was a surprise. Women from small towns were afraid the subway would swallow them up. Even women from Minnesota found the East Coast cold to be shocking.

Jaenn Magdalene Coz, a librarian from California, traveled east on a five-day troop train and alighted into ankle-deep New York snow wearing only her thin civilian clothes. She was left-handed but had been forced to use her right hand in school, so she had trouble discerning left from right, and this made marching difficult. On Christmas night, her unit was marching through wet slush and she felt so cold and homesick that she started to cry. As punishment for crying, she was made to mop the dirty snow from the hallways of the apartment building. During training, she asked to be sent back to California and stationed in San Francisco. She was sent to Washington, DC, to break codes instead.

The WAVES by mid-1943 were a big deal. New York mayor Fiorello La Guardia loved to watch the Hunter College women on parade. He would call at the last minute and say he wanted to bring an ambassador or other foreign dignitary, and the women would drop what they were doing and muster. There were reviews every Saturday morning, with a Navy brass band, a WAVES drum and bugle corps, and a color guard proudly carrying the blue flag of the USS Hunter.

It was not only women from outside New York who had their horizons expanded. Jane Case was the daughter of Theodore Case, a physicist who pioneered sound in movies and worked during World War I to develop the Navy's ship-to-shore communications. Jane grew up in a huge house in Auburn, New York, where she had been crushingly lonely. Her mother belittled Jane, making her conscious of her imperfections, for example, highlighting her nearsightedness by snatching the glasses off her face. Jane, to her relief, was sent away to the Chapin School in New York City. While she loved it there, she hated Manhattan high society. It was stuffy and boring. Pearl Harbor cut short her debutante season—a time when young women from high society were paraded about at balls and parties in the hopes that they would make a good marriage.

Jane had always had a visual mind and could see, in her mind's eye, the country from sea to shining sea, the United States and its people rolling out before her from east to west: mountains, wheat fields, rivers, Americans of all creeds and races. She found the vision of teeming diversity to be thrilling. As soon as the WAVES were created, Jane took the subway to Lower Manhattan to enlist. She memorized the eye chart and managed to make it through the eye examination without revealing that she wore glasses, which might have disqualified her for service.

Jane had expected to be made an officer, but the Navy did not consider her time at the Longy School of Music to be equal to two years of college. Jane did not object. It suited her fine to be an ordinary seaman. Families with a son in the service put stars in their windows to show their sacrifice and contribution. Jane obtained a star, slapped it down in front of her mother, and said, "There. There's nothing you can do about it." She joined the singing platoon at Hunter and loved it. In Washington, she bunked with a mortician's daughter who was very proud of a music box her father had given her, in the shape of a casket.

"I would have to look at it every day, and say, 'that's so beautiful!'"

Courtesy of U.S. Army INSCOM

Women rushed to enlist and help the war effort.

CHAPTER NINE

"Q for Communications"

December 1942

By late 1942, the Navy's Washington, DC, code-breaking operation—like that of the Army—had grown so large that it had to be relocated. In just under six months, the office had swelled from a few hundred to more than a thousand people. The Navy found a women's junior college in Washington's Tenleytown neighborhood. The school, Mount Vernon Seminary, occupied some thirty-eight acres on an elevated point from which it was possible to see the Pentagon in Virginia—even the Blue Ridge Mountains, beyond it—and Fort Meade in Maryland. On December 15, 1942, the Navy seized possession of its campus and buildings.

The Navy's top secret code-breaking operation was now located at 3801 Nebraska Avenue NW, a peaceful patch of land graced by trees and birdsong. Prior to the move, Navy leaders met to find a "harmless" cover name for the facility. In the end it was called the Naval Communications Annex, but most people called it the Annex, the USS Mount Vernon Seminary, or WAVES Barracks D. It was located near where Massachusetts and Nebraska Avenues converge at Ward Circle, which taxi drivers started calling WAVES Circle.

Rows of glorified Quonset huts were built to house the women across the street among the green lawns and big mansions of the neighborhood. Barracks D was the largest WAVES barracks—a primitive group of buildings put up quickly to house soldiers—in the world. Virtually all the women who lived there were code breakers. It soon had a beauty shop and a bowling alley. The women were assigned bunks and tall lockers. There was a mess hall catered by Hot Shoppes, a local cafeteria chain known for its milk shakes and hot fudge sundaes. The women worked round-the-clock shifts, which made it hard to sleep. There were always people coming and going.

There was a lot of curiosity in Washington about what went on at the Naval Communications Annex. The enlisted women were given a naval rating, Specialist Q, which was inscribed on a patch they wore on their uniforms. The Q did not stand for anything, but it did arouse a lot of curiosity.

One day, Jane Case, the former debutante, was walking up Wisconsin Avenue when a car stopped and offered her a ride. The wartime rule was that cars should pick up members of the military. It was pouring rain and Jane climbed into the back. The driver was a man wearing a raincoat, and his wife was sitting beside him. During the ride, he grilled Jane, asking her what went on in the communications annex and what she was doing for the Navy.

She replied with the answer she always had ready. "I fill inkwells and sharpen pencils and give people what they need," she told him.

"What does the Q in Specialist Q stand for?" he asked her.

Jane laughed it off. "It's Q for communications; you know, the Navy can't spell," she joked.

When they got to the barracks and the driver reached across and opened the back door to let her out, the sleeve of his raincoat hiked up slightly. Jane saw one gold stripe, and then several more. She realized that the driver was a Navy admiral. He gave her a faint, knowing smile. He had been testing her. She had passed.

Jane wasn't the only one to whom this sort of meeting happened. After arriving in Washington, Ruth Rather and some other WAVES were told they had a few days off before they began work. They were advised to see the sights. As they did so, they were struck by the number of male strangers who tried to strike up conversations with them. When they showed up for their first day at the Annex, they were introduced to the same men—naval officers who had been testing them.

─────────

At Mount Vernon the Navy women now worked in every unit. Women's ranks would grow until there were four thousand women breaking enemy naval codes at the USS Mount Vernon Seminary, making up 80 percent of the total workforce there.

For the women, being in the know about the message content was eye-opening. By early 1943 many US citizens were led to believe America was winning the war, or starting to. This was not wrong, necessarily, but the code breakers understood the full cost.

When Ensign Marjorie Faeder reported for duty, she found herself assigned to work the noisy, rugged piece of equipment used for transmitting and receiving American messages. The "incoming messages were telling us very clearly that we were losing the war in the Pacific," she later remembered. "Casualties were high, ships were going down, subs were lost." Faeder found the difference between the public news and the private truth shocking.

Some of the male commanders did not see the women as proper sailors, but as they went about their assignments, the women found skills within themselves they had not known existed. Jane Case—told, growing up, that she was bad at math—discovered that wasn't true. She sat at a desk in a large room where a conveyor belt brought messages to her; it was her job to use her math skills to evaluate a few enciphered numbers at the beginning and decide which JN-25 messages were important enough to pass on. She was very careful in making decisions. An error in judgment could be catastrophic. The work demanded hard, intense, constant focus. That was stressful. There were far too many messages to break every one. Working in land-locked northwest Washington, DC, Jane could tell if a major Pacific Fleet action was under way, because the stack would grow even higher. "Because of the traffic you knew something big was happening."

As the men in the war theater did their brave and grisly work, the women at the Annex did their best to support them. After a long slog through sand and jungle, the United States secured Guadalcanal in the western Pacific in February 1943. Guadalcanal was the chief island in the Solomon Islands. The Japanese had captured it in July 1942, and promptly began building an airfield. This airfield would give Japanese planes easy access to Australia, a

US ally. Securing the island became critical for the Allies. The US Marines landed on Guadalcanal in August 1942. The fighting continued for the next six months, before the Japanese evacuated in February 1943.

From Guadalcanal it was on to the Gilbert Islands, the Marshalls, and the Marianas: Saipan, Guam, Tinian. In advance of every push, every landing, the tempo in the code-breaking rooms would speed up. Days off, called furloughs, would be canceled. The women were told to give no hint, outside the office, of the quickened pace within it—not even in other parts of the Annex.

The additive recovery unit had received a commendation for its work during the Guadalcanal campaign. Their top boss, Commander Charles Ford, wanted more than 2,500 additives recovered in the course of a day. The women obliged, and then some. They broke their own record, with 2,563 additives recovered on one day.

The women quickly rose to trusted positions. Many female officers who started out as ensigns became lieutenants junior grade, which was the next rank up, and then full lieutenants, and sometimes lieutenant commanders.

As American forces assaulted enemy-held islands in the Pacific, the US men were sometimes able to capture codebooks left by retreating forces. Betty Hyatt was on duty in 1944 when a naval officer brought in a Japanese codebook.

The fact that it was recovered was important and had to be kept top secret so that the Japanese wouldn't suspect and change their codes once again. The officer traveled as an ordinary businessman so that his trip would go unnoticed. The codebook was up-to-date and intact but for some slightly burned pages. It identified code groups in the latest version of JN-25 and enabled the code breakers to read every message on file in that system. Betty volunteered to help, an exhausting job that took two days and two sleepless nights. The code, she later recalled, "gave them the location of Japanese ships, what was on each, who was on each, and the station."

During this effort Betty was assigned to take some code recoveries to a high-priority room, where she opened a door and was shocked to see a man waiting to receive it who was Japanese. She stood in the doorway, paralyzed and uncertain what to do. Every American citizen by then had heard the most intense and cruel propaganda against Japanese people. "We had been taught that anything Oriental is your enemy and you cannot trust them," as she later put it. The women had been warned that "this place could be invaded at any moment." Clearly the worst had happened, Betty thought, and the enemy had seized the Naval Annex. Determined to hold out to the last, Betty refused to surrender the material she was holding. The man laughed graciously.

"I'm an American," he assured her. He was a Nisei, an American citizen of Japanese heritage, working as a translator.

"You don't look like one," she blurted in her exhaustion, and felt sorry about that hurtful, racist remark for the rest of her life.

Despite being so dependent upon women—women who were doing excellent work—the Navy still had some false ideas about them. They feared that so many women could not resist gossiping about their work, especially to their good friends. So the Navy developed strategies—such as moving women from barracks to barracks—to prevent them from forming close friendships. The tactic failed. Completely.

Scores of women worked in the library unit, where about a dozen formed a tight friendship. The library unit typed incoming messages on file cards, categorizing them and making careful note of coincidences and recurrences. Like the women in additive recovery, they responded to action in the war theater. When Betty Allen, a librarian from a small Illinois town, arrived in the unit, she became a staunch member of the friendship group. So did Georgia O'Connor, a farm girl from Missouri; Lyn Ramsdell, who had worked in the office of a Boston wool merchant; and Ruth Schoen, a legal secretary.

Ruth Schoen was the only Jewish member of the group. Her grandparents on both sides had emigrated from Hungary. Like most Americans, she was not yet aware of the Nazi death camps, but she was patriotic and wanted to do her part so badly that she enlisted despite being underweight and underage. An excellent student, she skipped a grade and graduated from high school at seventeen. She wanted to go to college, but her parents told her she needed to supplement the family income. Part of her earnings went to pay her brother's college tuition. She herself enrolled in night classes at Brooklyn College. Enlisting in June 1943, she picked the Navy because her father had served in it in World War I. Being underage, she needed a parent's consent. Her father would not give it, but her mother did. A pound too light for the Navy's standards, she ate as much as she could and managed to pass their tests.

Of all the women in the library group, Ruth was the one whose family lived the closest, and she would invite her new friends to travel home with her for visits. "My parents were so happy" to host the women, she said. They loved them all and made sure to find the churches they wanted to attend on Sunday. "They treated us like a nest of chicks," Lyn Ramsdell remembered.

In Washington, there was a synagogue that had weekly Friday night parties, and toward the end of 1943 Ruth met a soldier there named Dave Mirsky. They dated a bit, and at some point Dave's brother Harry came to visit him. When Dave was sent overseas with a unit of tank destroyers, Harry Mirsky took his brother's place courting Ruth. All the women in the library unit loved Harry Mirsky. He had been injured when thrown from a jeep and so was still stateside, recovering. "Guess who's waiting for you downstairs!" they would tease Ruth, coming in as she was finishing her shift. On their dates he would sometimes ask her what she did, and she would change the subject. After two months Harry took Ruth to dinner and told her, abruptly, "I want you to be my wife."

"I hardly know you," she protested.

"I've made up my mind," he replied. They met in December 1944 and married in May 1945. Her friends threw her a shower in a French restaurant. Ruth applied for permission to wear a wedding gown, which was considered civilian clothing. She had six days of leave in which to find a dress, arrange the ceremony, marry, and take a Catskills honeymoon. All of her Specialist Q librarian friends managed to get to Queens for the wedding. Some were granted leave; some took a chance and went briefly AWOL.

Georgia O'Connor was next in the group to marry. Despite having grown up poor, she married a wealthy heir to a publishing fortune, a man whose wartime job was tracking Nazi spies in Chicago and whose family owned a villa near Cannes that was now occupied by Germans. When her high-society mother-in-law asked what her own father did for a living, Georgia O'Connor replied, honestly, "He slops pigs."

This kind of thing happened all the time. Amid the wartime upheaval, pairings that might have been unthinkable before the war became normal.

The women were living life in the moment, with little idea what the future held.

Arlington Hall, the former girls' finishing school that had been converted to a massive code-breaking facility with more than seven thousand workers—most of them female.

CHAPTER TEN

MacArthur's Secret Weapon

April 1943

Young Annie Caracristi washed her hair with laundry soap. Wilma Berryman, the West Virginia schoolteacher who had been one of William Friedman's early hires, felt sure of it. Shampoo, like so many items, was not always easy to come by in wartime. Annie's hair was thick and curly and flew everywhere.

Blue-eyed, blond, and friendly, Ann Caracristi came to work at Arlington Hall each day wearing bobby socks, flat shoes, and a pleated skirt. She looked like a carefree college girl who lived for boyfriends and swing dances. But appearances were deceiving. General Douglas MacArthur did not know it, but one of his secret weapons was this twenty-three-year-old from Bronxville, New York. Intellectually ferocious, Annie worked twelve-hour shifts, day after day.

Annie Caracristi surprised everybody, most of all herself, with her cryptanalytic feats. Though she had been an English major in college, she had the mind of an engineer. It was fascinating for Wilma Berryman—now supervising a major unit at Arlington Hall—to see what Annie could do. Nothing the Japanese did could shake her off. Wilma made Ann the head of her research group.

The Army's code-breaking operation at Arlington Hall was open-minded. Anybody could be in charge of anything. Men and women of different ages and backgrounds worked side by side at its wooden tables. Which is not to say that there wasn't sexism. One of the men referred to Arlington Hall's southern workers as the "Jewels." It was a snide reference to the number of women whose parents had named them after precious stones. In addition to Opals and Pearls, the workforce included a real Jewel—Jewel Hogan. And there was Jeuel Bannister, a band director recruited out of South Carolina.

At Arlington Hall there also were "BIJs," or born-in-Japans, the term for people who grew up in missionary families and worked in the translating section. There was also a group of siblings and cousins—the Erskines—who had relocated as a family unit from Ohio. There were nannies, beauticians, secretaries, restaurant hostesses, and a future billionaire. Josephine Palumbo at eighteen was virtually running the personnel unit. The daughter of an Italian immigrant laborer, she was the person who swore in newcomers.

Unlike the Navy, Arlington Hall also had an African American code-breaking unit. Eleanor Roosevelt—or somebody at the top—had declared that 12 to 15 percent of the Arlington Hall workforce should be black. Arlington Hall's African American workers had to take segregated streetcars and buses to get there, and even college graduates were given jobs as janitors and messengers. But there also was a special code-breaking unit. The African American unit monitored the enciphered communications of companies and banks to see what was being talked about and who was doing business in Germany or in Japan. There was no shortage of qualified people to staff the unit. The city of Washington had a number of highly regarded black public schools, as well as Howard, one of the country's premier historically black universities. One of the team members, Annie Briggs, started out as a secretary and rose to head the production unit. Another, Ethel Just, led the expert translators. William Coffee, a black man who studied English at Knoxville College in Tennessee, started out as a janitor and waiter at Arlington Hall and rose to lead the whole team.

Despite the important work they did, the black code-breaking unit was unknown to most of Arlington Hall's white workers and wasn't celebrated after the war.

———

The atmosphere at Arlington Hall was unlike anything the US military had ever produced. Physically, the place was a hodgepodge. The main schoolhouse retained its Old Virginia flavor, but the new temporary buildings were purely functional. Building A—where the Purple cipher was attacked along with other ciphers—consisted of two floors and a basement with a fireproof vault. Designed to hold 2,200 people, it quickly proved to be too small, and so B was built. Soon the campus boasted a beauty parlor, a tailor, a barbershop, a clinic with fourteen beds, a 620-seat auditorium and theater, a mess hall, a car repair shop, a warehouse, and a recreation building. The two main buildings were chilly in winter and sweltering hot in summer.

Feeding the workforce was a challenge. At first there were box lunches; then a cafeteria was created and replaced by an even bigger one. Demand was so high that both were kept up and running. The snack bar stayed open most of the night, so people on the graveyard shift could eat.

Transportation was also a challenge. Bus drivers and buses were in short supply. Employees had to display badges with photos and a color denoting their clearance level to enter the site. If a code breaker forgot her badge, she had to wear a "forgot my badge" badge. One version displayed the cartoon face of a donkey.

There was plenty of evidence that a real war was going on. Military officers headed many units, and enlisted men came in and out. Even among the soldiers, though, rank had little meaning. A lieutenant might report to a sergeant or a civilian or even a private. If the officer objected, he was sent overseas. "You didn't go by rank," said Solomon Kullback, an early William Friedman hire. "You went by what people knew."

The same was true of women. It would be an exaggeration to say women enjoyed true equality at Arlington Hall. Among the early William Friedman hires, men like Frank Rowlett, Abraham Sinkov, and Solomon Kullback were awarded military commissions, but the veteran women were not promoted in the same way. Even so, all of the early women—Wilma Berryman, Delia Taylor, Genevieve Grotjan—found themselves running top units.

In part this was thanks to the open-mindedness of the people in charge, but it was also thanks to their desperation. In the early months of 1943, Arlington Hall struggled to make headway in one of the Pacific War's most urgent challenges: breaking the codes of the Imperial Japanese

Army. In this effort, it was Wilma Berryman and Ann Caracristi who would make the first significant break.

The Army's code-breaking unit had its hands full keeping up with Purple, as well as the codes and ciphers of many enemy and neutral nations. But the Army's toughest assignment continued to be breaking Imperial Japanese Army codes. These were separate from those of the Imperial Japanese Navy and—this long into the war—remained unbroken.

Part of the problem, at first, had been a lack of message traffic. Before the war, the Japanese Army had two million troops stationed in China and on the Manchurian border. These units were close enough to Japan that they could use low-frequency, low-power transmissions, and the US Army had a hard time getting radio intercepts. To break a complex code like the ones used by the Japanese military, it's essential to have lots and lots of intercepted messages.

In 1941, in the panicked atmosphere after Pearl Harbor, a British colleague had brought some Japanese Army intercepts to Friedman's operation. Friedman shut Solomon Kullback, Wilma Berryman, Delia Taylor, and Abraham Sinkov in a room, telling them not to come out until they had broken something. The job was just too big.

After about three months, Solomon Kullback stood up and shoved his desk back into the German section. The only positive outcome was that Delia Taylor and Abe Sinkov fell in love, got married, and moved into a houseboat. Other than that, the winter of 1942 was a gloomy one.

Success was the Japanese Army's undoing. After its stunning victories in the first half of 1942, the Japanese Army began to spread out. Japanese units fanned out over Asia and the Pacific archipelagos. Each unit remained tied to its home base in Japan and sent back reports. As the Japanese Army got farther from Japan, radiomen increased the power of their transmissions, and this made it possible to intercept them.

Soon enough, Japanese Army messages began pouring into Arlington Hall by the tens of thousands. But there were many different code systems, each complicated in its own way. In the final months of 1942 and into early 1943, the code breakers of Arlington Hall worked in a fever—painfully aware that their colleagues in the US Navy had broken JN-25.

After the US success at the Battle of Midway, America was forming a plan to push back. The Army and Navy agreed that the Navy, under Admiral Chester Nimitz, would deploy mostly in the central and North Pacific, a huge arena where the only land was tiny atolls. In the southwestern part of the hemisphere, the US Army—led by General Douglas MacArthur—would fight along the islands.

MacArthur's goal was to retake the Philippines and invade Japan. Operation Cartwheel called for the US Army and Navy to work together. As MacArthur's Army troops made beach landings and fought a fierce, dug-in island enemy, Navy admiral William "Bull" Halsey would support them from ships in the South Pacific. The Army faced months, maybe years, of beach and jungle warfare. The soldiers needed intelligence to tell them where the enemy's troops were.

For a code breaker, no situation is more stressful than knowing lives depend on you. If you crack the code, people will live. If you don't, they may die. A new unit was set up to break the Japanese Army systems, led by Frank Lewis, one of Friedman's most brilliant hires. Lewis, the Utah-bred son of an Englishman turned cowboy, was a gifted musician, a lover of puns, and a puzzle enthusiast. Friedman's top women also worked the Japanese Army problem. They worked on the hot upper floors of the old schoolhouse in rooms so crowded that it wasn't unusual to find an exhausted code breaker napping in a bathtub.

Matching wits against an unseen enemy, their little band was vastly outnumbered.

As the Japanese Army spread out around the Pacific, its cryptographers created new code systems and subdivided old ones. The Japanese created a host of minor codes and at least four major four-digit systems: one for ground forces, another for air forces, another for high-level administrators, and another for the "water transport organization." This was a lifeline of marus, or commercial merchant ships, that carried oil, food, and equipment to the captured islands.

It was a huge tangle of systems, and as of January 1943 there were just fifteen American civilians, twenty-three officers, and twenty-eight enlisted men working on breaking all of them.

At Arlington Hall, code breakers including Ann Cara-cristi (far right) matched wits against Japanese code makers.

CHAPTER ELEVEN

"That's It! That's It!"

April 1943

One of the civilians working to break the huge number of Japanese Army codes was Annie Caracristi, the twenty-three-year-old who washed her hair with laundry soap. She had been recruited out of Russell Sage, a women's college in Troy, New York. Her father died while Ann was in her teens, but she was able to attend college thanks to a friend of her mother's. Annie played basketball and edited both the campus newspaper and the literary magazine.

In May 1942, the Army Signal Corps had met with representatives from twenty colleges, including Dr. Bernice Smith from Russell Sage. The dean later told Ann and two classmates that there were jobs in Washington for women with brains and imagination. The three friends traveled down after graduation, taking rooms in a Wyoming Avenue boardinghouse. Soon enough, Ann found herself working at Arlington Hall. She started by sorting intercepts to be typed up and put onto IBM punch cards so that code groups could be compared.

Progress was slow. To the naked eye, the major Japanese Army code systems consisted of an unbroken string of four-digit numbers. The code breakers knew only that the systems were enciphered codes, somewhat like JN-25, involving both a code and an additive book. But the Arlington Hall team could not figure out the encipherment method. Despite attack after attack, they were stuck.

They decided to see if they could crack even just the address that began every message. This was a series of only a half dozen or so code groups, but they were important ones. After a Japanese Army message was enciphered, it passed to a radioman who attached an address specifying who the message was from (the *hatsu*), who it was going to (the *chiya*), and where those people and their units were located (the *ate*, or address). The address designated the Army command, installation, or officer for whom the message was intended.

Details like that provide intelligence about the makeup and location of enemy forces. The address was in its own code system, used only by the radiomen and different from that of the message itself. If Arlington Hall could break the address code, it would tell them who in the Japanese Army was where. It also might provide clues that could help the code breakers get into the messages themselves.

Wilma Berryman was assigned to the address problem in April 1942, and in June, Ann Caracristi joined the group. Ann and Wilma formed an immediate bond. It was an unlikely pairing: Wilma was a down-home West Virginian who liked to call people "honey" and to use adjectives like "stinkin'." Ann was ten years younger, a northerner, uncertain yet of her own abilities, and inexperienced. The two women shared high spirits, humor, brains, imagination, and a determination to succeed.

The women tried a number of approaches. Ann was assigned to do something called "chaining" differences, which is a long, agonizing process that involves subtracting one code group from another with the hope that two code groups might have been enciphered with the same additive. Chaining differences is code breaking the hard way, a method used when there are no other clues.

They had caught a small break when a Japanese plane crashed in Burma; the British captured some message templates—blank forms with some code groups filled in to speed the process—and sent them to Arlington Hall. Wilma and Ann began having conversations about how best to use this material in late January 1943 when they had them in their hands.

They had also received a report from Australia with some names and ID numbers for Japanese Army units in the southwest Pacific. In addition, the US Navy had sent over some cribs. At times, the Japanese Army was obliged to send messages over Navy radio circuits. In that event, a naval address code was added. The naval address was in a simple code that had been solved.

The Arlington Hall address team had well-kept records, and Wilma Berryman remembered some Japanese Army messages with addresses that might be the same as these Navy ones. She found them and began fiddling around, writing the plain words from the Navy address codes below the Army ciphers. "I sort of remembered having seen something in that file and I went back to the file and found it," was how she put it later. "I found what I thought looked like it ought to be that, the same thing. I had it on my desk and I just wasn't positive."

Suddenly she noticed one of the men who worked with their unit, Al Small, standing behind her. He asked her what she was doing. She told him and he stood there for a long time, watching.

"You've got it," he said finally. "That's it! That's it!"

Her solution was Arlington Hall's first real break

into any Japanese Army system. In early February 1943, a memo reported that "with the aid of the captured messages it has been possible to read the first encoded and enciphered addresses." It would be followed by months of careful work. Enciphered codes do not yield to immediate solutions like machine ciphers do. The code breakers had to build a bank of additives and figure out what each code group stood for.

Arlington Hall began producing weekly memos to keep the Pentagon and others updated. On March 15, 1943, a memo reported that more address code values were emerging. Ann, Wilma, and their few colleagues were beginning to recover additives and to understand the system's unique sum check. Like the Japanese Navy, the Japanese Army cryptographers were fond of sum checks as a guard against garble, but they had devised a method different from the "divisible by three" sum check of the Japanese Navy. In this system, the four-digit code groups were actually three digits, plus a fourth digit that served as a sum check. If a code group was 0987, for example, 098 was the actual code group, and 7 (using false math) was the sum check: $0 + 9 + 8 = 7$.

Reconstructing an enemy codebook is called "book-breaking," and Ann Caracristi turned out to be stunningly good at it. By summer 1943, they dug out the code groups for Hiroshima, Singapore, Kupang, and Tokyo.

The work that Ann Caracristi and Wilma Berryman were doing enabled US military intelligence to construct what is called the order of battle: an accounting of the strength, equipment, kind, and location of Japanese Army troops. Soon "MacArthur's headquarters had as good a picture of the Japanese military set-up as he had of his own," as Solomon Kullback put it. As it grew in importance, the address unit grew in number.

Wilma's team, which was 100 percent female, worked alongside a mostly female unit called "traffic analysis." It was the job of traffic analysis to follow changes in Japanese Army message traffic, without worrying about the actual message content. If a flurry of radio messages began going back and forth to a new location, this meant somebody was on the move. Before long, Wilma would find someone from military intelligence standing behind her, telling her which addresses to concentrate on. Arlington Hall began to produce a daily order-of-battle summary.

For the women code breakers, it was exhilarating. The same address code was appended to all the different Japanese Army systems, so soon enough every kind of message—air force, administrative, water transport, ground troops—was passing through their hands. "I think that's one of the things that made it so much fun. We saw everything, everything had to come through us," Wilma later said. "You had cryptanalysis, you had traffic analysis, and you had order of battle, and you could hardly ask for a better job. You were sitting right on top of the world and you were following the Japs all over hell's half-acre, all the time.... I thought it was the most exciting job in the place."

Courtesy of Library of Congress

Women poured into DC's Union Station, which now offered a servicemen's canteen, an information desk for new government workers, and posters and flags attesting to the country's determination to win. This photo is by Gordon Parks, a government photographer at the time.

CHAPTER TWELVE

A Major Break

July 1943

Staying up-to-date with Japanese Army codes was a never-ending job. As with the Navy, the Japanese Army regularly changed both its books and its methods. There was a grim period when the radiomen began using one method to encipher addresses that had an odd number of code groups, and another method to encipher those with an even number. The address unit seemed on the verge of collapse.

"They had been getting such beautiful order of battle, and all of a sudden, just like that, it was wiped out," Wilma Berryman later recalled. "And so we had to do something about it."

Even in this elite group of code breakers, Ann Caracristi was in a class by herself. Wilma put Ann in charge of a small research team that included a mathematician named Anne Solomon and a male Harvard graduate, Ben Hazard, who had a physical condition that disqualified him from service.

As the Americans began to retake Pacific islands, the Japanese had a hard time distributing new codebooks to isolated outposts. Often the Japanese cryptographers had to create a solution using old books in a new way. The Japanese would make squares, in which they would take additives from the old book, and—rather than adding them—run them vertically and horizontally to construct a square table. Squares are hard to break. But there were patterns, and Ann's training included some preparation for breaking squares.

What the Japanese were doing was encryption, and what Ann and her team were able to do, over and over, was unlock the encryption. They would work through the night to recover a key.

Years later, when Solomon Kullback was asked whom he would want if he were stranded on a desert island and only one person could crack the message that would get him home, he didn't hesitate: "Ann Caracristi."

In the long-running beef between the US Army and Navy, one of the Navy's objections was that, by hiring a civilian workforce, the Army was likely to hire reckless people who could not keep a secret. This could not have been farther from the truth. A violation of the secrecy oath carried a fine of $10,000 or ten years in prison. But the civilians took the secrecy oath in earnest. When Ann was asked what she did at Arlington Hall, she talked about clerical work.

The code breakers preferred not to have to explain things at all. The easiest way was to hang out with one another. The top Japanese Army code breakers ate lunch together and dined in the few local restaurants. Ann and Wilma and a few others even bought a sailboat together. The code breakers also formed a glee club and a theater group, played tennis, and set up bowling in the alleys of Clarendon and Colonial Village, two nearby neighborhoods.

There were love affairs, and there were deep and abiding friendships. But mostly there was work. The goal was not to seek advancement. The goal was to serve the war effort. All this, they knew, was temporary. The point was to win the war and get back to their regularly scheduled lives.

There was competition—with the Navy, with the British, with a small US code-breaking outpost in Australia, with one another—but the point was just to get a solution first. They couldn't get people to stop working. There was a huge snowstorm, and everybody managed to walk to work. This was the spirit that led to the next major break, one that was as important as the Battle of Midway.

Breaking the address code was a vital achievement, but the main Japanese Army codes were still unsolved. By the spring of 1943, the situation was grim. The staff at Arlington Hall, along with their companion unit in Australia, began concentrating on the system known as 2468, the "water-transport code" used by the Japanese Army to route its supply ships, or marus. The team knew that 2468 was an enciphered code and that buried somewhere in each message were two four-digit groups that made up the indicator. The indicator told which part of the additive book had been consulted. The indicator was the central clue, and people all over the world were working to find it. As late as March 1943, the effort felt hopeless.

Then in April, the Arlington Hall unit received a telegram from England that mentioned a peculiar aspect of 2468: In the second code group of each message, the first digit did not seem random. A second telegram, from Australia, confirmed and elaborated on that finding. Any digit in the first position of the third code group shared a relationship with the corresponding digit of the second group: If the latter was 0, then the other would be 2, 4, or 9.

With this breakthrough, the Arlington Hall code breakers began to look at the code in a new way. Around midnight on April 6 and going into the wee hours of April 7, an elite team shut themselves in a room and put a sign on the door barring anybody else from entering. The digits, they finally realized, lined up in a pattern.

They had broken a complex and crucial system. The indicator consisted of two four-digit code groups. The first indicator group provided, in its first digit, the number of the additive book used. The second two digits gave the page number, and the fourth digit was a sum check. The second indicator group gave the page's row and column.

But here was the truly diabolical part. The message was enciphered, and then used to further encipher the indicators. It was an incredibly complicated system, like a Russian nesting doll with layers upon layers of ciphers.

The feeling inside Arlington Hall was electric. Several problems that seemed impossible to solve could now be attacked because of what was proved in 2468. The code breakers were able to use the word "maru," which appeared often, to recover additives. Then they proceeded to break other systems. As the Japanese Eighth Area Army split around Rabaul in Papua New Guinea, it began sending identical messages, enciphered by the same additive but using different squares, to different units. The code breakers could compare duplicates to tease out additives.

It didn't take long to feel the import of what they had

done. In July 1943, one of the first 2468 messages broken by Arlington Hall revealed that there would soon be four marus in Wewak Harbor. Wewak, on the island of New Guinea, was the site of a major Japanese air base. The code breakers passed this information to military intelligence. Not long after, Solomon Kullback was listening to the war news on a local radio station and heard that the US Navy had sunk four marus in Wewak Harbor.

The break into 2468 was one of the most important of the war. It was every bit as important as the breaking of Enigma or the Midway triumph. The 2468 code routed nearly every single maru making its way around the Pacific to supply the Japanese Army. As with Japanese Navy vessels, many marus sent a daily message giving the exact location where they would be at noon. The information would be turned over to American sub commanders.

The US military used tricks so the Japanese wouldn't know the maru sinkings were the result of a broken code. American planes would be sent up so it would look as though they had spotted the maru from the air. The Japanese sent messages saying they thought spies along the island coasts were to blame, which the Arlington Hall code breakers read with glee.

Now that Arlington Hall had cracked 2468, they wanted to crack every Japanese Army system. The solution of 2468 led to breaks in code systems called 5678, 2345, 6666, and 7777. They solved 3366, an aviation code, and 6789, which dealt with promotions and transfers, pay and requests for funding, troop movements, and reports from the "hygiene bureau," telling how many Japanese soldiers were dead and wounded, how many sick from typhus and other diseases. They knew not only the enemy's location and pay but also his state of health. This kind of information let the United States know where the enemy was weakest. Soldiers with typhus and other diseases didn't have the energy to fight.

Arlington Hall had become one big communal brain. For weeks a major administrative code, 7890, seemed unbreakable. Then one day, a lieutenant working on the team started chatting with Frank Lewis about it. The lieutenant wondered whether it might be enciphered using the kind of square that some other systems employed. Lewis said that if that was the case, they could expect certain numbers to start showing up, like 9939.

Delia Taylor Sinkov overheard them. She pointed out that 9939 was the most frequent group in the 5678 system. It was this chance conversation that broke the administrative code. This system gave them intelligence that included the numbers of Japanese soldiers killed and wounded, and, at least once, information about a major planned attack.

Arlington Hall eventually broke every code they came up against. They read messages even before the Japanese recipients did. That was exactly what the Japanese were afraid of. The code breakers knew that in the Japanese Army, punishment for a lost or captured codebook was so severe that soldiers often would not admit a codebook had gone missing. In January 1944, Australian soldiers found the entire cryptographic library of the Twentieth Division in New Guinea in a deep, water-filled pit. The codebooks were passed to Arlington Hall, where the code breakers used the materials to read messages a soldier sent to his superiors, assuring them of just how thoroughly he had destroyed the very books they were holding. The books provided intelligence that played a major role in MacArthur's campaigns in New Guinea and the Solomon Islands.

The address codes—whose solution had kicked everything off—continued to be essential. All intercepts would start out in Wilma Berryman's unit, where the address would be solved. Often, a single Japanese Army message was sent in eight or ten sections. The numbers, which were part of the address preamble, helped the staff members who were doing the message sorting to reassemble the pieces. Then it was on to the code-breaking unit.

It was still a small group of people reading the mail of the entire Japanese Army. By mid-1943, a select group of code-breaking veterans, some promising civilians including Ann Caracristi, and a handful of military men were dealing with all of the Purple messages and all of the Japanese Army codes.

If they were really going to assist the US military to win in its Pacific campaign, they had to "build an organization that would produce results as rapidly as possible," as one memo put it. That meant breaking down the work into smaller elements, developing a well-oiled assembly line—and hiring many more Jewels.

It was the 2468 breakthrough and the floodgates it opened that led to the recruitment of Virginia schoolteacher Dot Braden.

The Code Girls Generation

The women were of a unique generation. Many were born in 1920, the year when American women won the right to vote. There was a growing awareness of female potential and there were more opportunities for women. The exploits of Amelia Earhart and other women aviators all pointed to new freedoms. So did the work of women like Nellie Bly, a journalist who became famous for writing about the lives of women and the poor.

When these women were children, however, the Great Depression hit. Opportunity stopped, and progress reversed. Many women were fired so that what jobs remained could be given to men.

For the women who said yes, those secret letters got them out in the world. Living in the fast-growing nation's capital, the code breakers rented rooms, scrambled for housing, shared beds—two women who worked different shifts and used the same bed called it "hot-bedding"—and settled where they could find a place. The capital was full of odd little boardinghouses. Some bedrooms had only curtains on their doorways. Some landlords served collard greens and black-eyed peas to northerners who had never eaten southern food. From Washington they were able to jump on the train during a forty-eight-hour or seventy-two-hour leave and spend a weekend in New York or even Chicago.

In Washington, the women code breakers took buses and trolleys. They went to USO dances and concerts and were celebrated all over the city. They looked out for one another.

They suddenly had a break between being daughters and being wives. Their lives were forever changed by the work they did and the freedom they had during the war.

CHAPTER THIRTEEN

Twenty-Eight Acres of Girls

September 1943

Fresh out of her senior year at a Virginia women's college, Dot Braden was hired to teach at a public high school in Chatham, Virginia, in 1942. As in the rest of the country, virtually all the male teachers in the small school had signed up to fight. Female teachers quit their jobs to marry the men before they shipped out. So, at the beginning of 1942, nearly all of the teaching at Chatham High School had fallen, or so it felt, on twenty-two-year-old Dot.

In her first week, she found that she was the school's eleventh- and twelfth-grade English teacher, its first- and second-year French teacher, its ancient-history teacher, its civics teacher, its hygiene teacher, and its calisthenics teacher. That last responsibility mostly entailed "General

Braden" marching the senior girls back and forth from lunch.

Dot did all she was asked. When the physics teacher left, there was another panic and scramble. Dot unwisely mentioned that her graduation certificate qualified her to teach physics, and she became the advanced physics teacher on top of everything else. Five days a week, eight hours a day, Dot Braden ran from classroom to classroom. She was paid $900 a year, which would equal around $14,000 today.

Dot was used to hard work, but if anybody had asked her—and nobody did—she would have said that teaching anybody anything while America was at war in this way was impossible. "It was terrible," Dot recalled later. "I mean to tell you, they dumped everything on me."

Halfway through the year her roommate left to get married and Dot inherited her English composition classes. Why she did not quit then, she would have had a hard time explaining. But when the year's final bell sounded, Dot Braden packed her bags and went home to Lynchburg, Virginia.

"I am never going back to that school," she told her mother. "I am not. It will kill me. I'm just through with teaching and all that."

Dot's mother, Virginia, was raising four children on her own, and Dot's income helped. There were few other good jobs available. Local ads seeking female labor mostly wanted telephone operators, waitresses, housemaids, and—always—schoolteachers. But Virginia Braden didn't want her oldest daughter doing work she hated, so they agreed Dot would look for something else.

Sometime after that conversation, Dot's mother came home and said that government recruiters were set up at the Virginian Hotel and were looking for schoolteachers. Her mother didn't know what the job was, exactly. She made it sound mysterious, maybe a little bit like spying. The job was in Washington, DC, and it had something to do with the war.

Washington, DC! Dot Braden had never been to Washington. Like most people she knew, she had rarely left Virginia. She did not take vacations, except to visit family members. The only time she could remember leaving Virginia was when she and some friends had gone to West Point, in New York, for a dance with Army cadets.

Virginia Braden had grown up without much money and wanted her children to have better opportunities. Virginia had decided early on that Dot would attend Randolph-Macon Woman's College, located in the heart of Lynchburg.

Dot was happy to follow her mother's orders. Money was a problem, however. A local businessmen's club awarded her a scholarship that covered tuition, but there was book money to pay, and they didn't have it. Dot shut herself in her closet and cried. A generous uncle came to the rescue.

During her college years Dot worked at a florist shop and earned extra money grading physics papers. At Randolph-Macon, she found she was good at languages. She had begun taking Latin and French in the seventh grade and continued both in college. Speaking French was a challenge, but writing and reading it came as easy as sleeping.

———

Dot presented herself at the Virginian Hotel on September 4, 1943. War by now had taken over her city. All that summer, Lynchburg's morning and evening papers had been full of news about the state of the war in Europe and in the Pacific. Closer to home, the news was about butter supplies and ration coupons. Ads urged citizens to buy war stamps. Food columns taught readers how to make wedding cakes in a time of hasty ceremonies and sugar rationing.

Given the news, the presence of war recruiters in a hotel lobby did not seem at all strange. Entering the hotel, Dot found a man and a woman standing behind a table in the lobby. The recruiters seemed very interested in Dot's talent for languages and asked her to fill out an application. They told Dot to provide character references and to state whether she had family members serving in the military. Both brothers by now were in the service.

The recruiters told Dot they would be in touch, and she allowed herself to hope. The more she thought about it, the more she liked the idea of working in Washington and doing her part. Like every other American family, the Bradens were enthusiastic about helping the war effort. For Dot, working in the nation's capital would be exciting.

Just a few weeks later, a letter arrived informing Dot that she was invited to work for the US Army Signal Intelligence Service. She was expected to pay her own way to Washington, but she would be paid $1,620 a year (around $25,000 in today's dollars), almost double what she had made teaching school.

On October 11, 1943, Virginia Braden came to the Lynchburg train station to see her daughter off. One of Dot's aunts came as well, and both of the older women were crying. Dot was too nervous for tears. She was carrying her raincoat and umbrella, along with two small suitcases containing all the clothes she owned. The train was crowded. Gas was rationed, as were tires, and most people no longer drove long distances. Members of the military received seating preference, so civilians often had to stand, or sit on a suitcase in the aisle. Dot was lucky and found a seat near a boy she knew from high school. He was on his way to start military training and asked where she was headed. "I'm going to Washington to take a government job," replied Dot proudly. When he asked her what the job was, Dot had to admit that she did not know. There had been something on the form about "cryptography," but she had no idea what that word meant.

———————————

After several hours the train pulled into Washington's Union Station. As Dot stepped out of the train she could feel that the tempo here was more fast-paced than in her hometown. The fact of the world war was everywhere, as was the nation's determination to win. Above Dot's head was a big poster fluttering from the ceiling that declared, AMERICANS WILL ALWAYS FIGHT FOR LIBERTY.

Clutching her belongings, Dot followed a sign that said TAXICABS and hailed a cab for the first time in her life. She gave the driver the address she had been told to report to, then settled back in her seat with a sense of awe and nervous excitement. Out the window Dot glimpsed the dome of the US Capitol and the Washington Monument. Soon she could see the Lincoln Memorial.

There was American history, old and new, stretching

out on all sides as the cab carried her over the Potomac River and along a highway that skirted Arlington National Cemetery. Soon the river was behind her and they were plunging deeper into the Virginia suburbs. The ride went on, and on and on, and Dot began to worry that she would not be able to pay the fare when they got wherever it was that they were headed.

Finally, the taxi pulled up in front of one of the strangest places Dot had ever seen. Behind a screen of trees loomed a large school building surrounded by newer buildings. Two steel mesh fences encircled the entire compound, and each building had its own fence. Dot's main impression was of lots and lots of terrifying wire. On the other side of the fences, high-ranking military officers walked with purpose. And that's where Dot, a twenty-three-year-old ex-schoolteacher, was expected to go.

Dot paid the driver—it took almost all the money she had—and walked up to a gate. "I'm supposed to be here," she said, giving her name and watching the guard pick up a telephone. She was directed to the main building, where she opened the door and found, to her relief, that she was expected. She was at a place called Arlington Hall. Before the war, Arlington Hall had been a school for girls. Now it had been transformed into a government operation whose purpose was not clear. The presence of so many military officers made Dot realize that her new job must be even more important and serious than she had understood. The thought was intimidating.

Inside the main building, the French doors and elegant moldings of the girls' school were intact, as was the gracious central staircase, but the furnishings consisted of no-nonsense chairs and desks. A self-assured civilian woman, no older than Dot, possibly younger, seemed to be in charge of the whole place.

Other women gathered in the hallway looking as uncertain as Dot felt. When a crowd had collected, the women were shown into a room where the self-assured young woman distributed copies of a loyalty oath. Dot signed it, swearing that she would "support and defend the Constitution of the United States against all enemies, foreign and domestic." She also signed a secrecy oath, swearing that she would not discuss her activities with anyone outside her official duties—not now, and not ever. If she did, she could be prosecuted under the Espionage Act. The whole exercise felt frightening. The self-assured young woman told Dot that was enough for the day. She could leave and come back tomorrow.

"There are buses here that will take you wherever you are staying," she said.

Dot looked blank. "Where I'm staying?"

"Aren't you staying somewhere?" the woman wanted to know.

"No, I'm not staying anywhere," Dot stammered, embarrassed. She had formed the idea—or had been led to believe—that the US government would provide lodging in return for her wartime service. She had been mistaken. There was nobody with whom she could stay; she did not know a soul in the city of Washington or its suburbs.

The woman told Dot that there was a place nearby where she could rent a room. Dot gathered her things and climbed onto a bus. In fifteen or twenty minutes she found herself standing on yet another campus. The female-only dormitories here were new and ugly. They had been built at the request of First Lady Eleanor Roosevelt. Young women like Dot were pouring into Washington to take jobs to serve the war effort, and they all needed a place to live.

Like Arlington Hall, these dormitories were located in Arlington County, Virginia, across the Potomac River from Washington. The women's dorms, wedged on a patch of land near the river, were intended to last only for the length of the war. They were so flimsy that whoever built them must have thought the war would be short.

Until recently the US Department of Agriculture had maintained an "experimental farm" on the same property.

That's how it came to be called Arlington Farms. But there were other, informal names for the sprawling new women's residence. In Washington, Arlington Farms was fast becoming known as Girl Town.

Other locals dubbed it "28 Acres of Girls."

Dot Braden (front, middle) as a young girl.

Many new arrivals rented tiny rooms at Arlington Farms dormitory in Virginia, built to house seven thousand women workers. Government photographer Esther Bubley documented their lives.

CHAPTER FOURTEEN

The Largest Clandestine Message Center in the World

October 1943

A nervous Dot Braden approached the front desk at Arlington Farms to ask for a room. A clerk told her that one was available in Idaho Hall, but she would have to pay a month's rent—$24.50—in advance. Dot didn't have that much money with her, and wouldn't until she got her first paycheck. She went into a phone booth and placed a long-distance call to her mother. "I've got to pay in advance," she told Virginia Braden.

"Well, I've never heard of anything like that in my whole life," came her mother's familiar voice.

"Well, Momma, that's what they say," she said. Dot felt guilty; she had taken the job to ease her mother's financial hardship, and here she was, making it even worse.

"Well, I'll find the money and send it to you," her mother told her, and that was that.

Arlington Farms had ten dorms in all, named after American states. Each one housed about seven hundred women. There was a cafeteria for meals, and women could send their clothes out to be laundered or dry-cleaned. Maids cleaned their rooms weekly.

Dot's dorm, Idaho Hall, had a lobby and lounges where the women could play cards, dance, drink tea, or sit with the soldiers and sailors who were always coming to visit. There was a recreation room, a shop, and a mail desk where women could pick up and mail letters.

Women were everywhere—some of them young, about Dot's age, but some of them as old as thirty or even forty. Dot found her way to Room I-106 and opened the door to find a tiny single furnished room with a bed, a desk, a mirror, two pillows, a chair, a wastebasket, and a window. Down the hall were a communal bathroom and showers. There were ironing boards and a kitchenette on every floor. Murals on the walls prettified what was essentially a barracks, flimsy buildings thrown up quickly to house soldiers. Only now those "soldiers" were women, mostly civilians.

In the morning Dot took the bus back to the fenced-in compound and found herself again in a crowd of women. None had any idea why they were here. As they milled about waiting for instructions, Dot chatted with a woman named Liz, who was from Durham, North Carolina.

"I'm going to stick with you," Liz said. "You look like you know what you're doing."

Dot had to laugh. She had been in Washington for twenty-four hours and still felt as confused as she had when she arrived. She was photographed from the front and the side holding a sign that said DOROTHY V. BRADEN and the number 7521. The photo was affixed to a badge, and the badge allowed her to enter certain parts of the compound.

During several days of orientation, Dot listened to lectures about the need for absolute secrecy around the work she would be doing. She visited rooms and workspaces where the activity gave her an inkling of what "cryptography" entailed. She went back to her single room each night with the dawning awareness that, as bizarre and unlikely as it might sound, she, Dot Braden, had been hired to break enemy codes.

Dot was to spend the bulk of her time in Building B, a low two-story building behind the main schoolhouse. Like the dorm where she was staying, her new workplace was designed in a style that might be called "temporary wartime Washington."

Inside, rooms were crammed with people—almost all women—working with graph paper, cards, pencils, and sheets of paper. Some sat at desks, but most were working at tables. Dot had never seen so many women side by side. No one person seemed to be in charge, and yet the women at the tables seemed to know what they were doing. Some tables were piled with stacks of cards and papers. Others had thin strips of paper hung from lines, like drying pasta. Lined up against walls were boxes and file cabinets. The cabinets were wooden, metal ones having been sacrificed to the war effort. It was not as quiet as a library, not as noisy as, say, a cafeteria; instead, there was a sort of constant low murmur. Dot didn't know this, but she had found her way into the largest clandestine message center in the world.

Everywhere women were attacking enemy messages pouring in via airmail, cable, and teletype. The messages originated in Nazi Germany, Japan, Italy, occupied France, Saudi Arabia, Argentina, even neutral countries like Switzerland. They were sent between top political leaders and military commanders. At the Allied listening stations where the messages were secretly intercepted, American operators further encrypted them using their own encoding machines. Once they got to Arlington Hall, the messages had to be stripped of the American encryption before they could be stripped of the enemy encryption.

The whole thing was hugely complex.

Technically, Arlington Hall was a military base, known as Arlington Hall Station. Dot could see that there were thousands of people working here. The ranks included a small number of Army officers and enlisted men, and some male civilians, including older professors and young men with disabilities that disqualified them for military service. But by far the majority were female civilians, and most of those, like Dot, were ex-schoolteachers.

Already, teachers were turning out to be well suited for code-breaking work. The qualities that made for a good code breaker were hard to know at first. Some PhDs were hopeless, and some high school dropouts were naturals. Code breaking required skill with words and numbers, creativity, painstaking attention to detail, a good memory, and a willingness to take guesses. It required a tolerance for boredom as well as energy and optimism.

Arlington Hall officials had found that problems based on "reasoning" and "word meanings" provided some insight into who might do well. Those who scored high on arithmetic tests often did well too. Hobbies, especially artistic hobbies, were another good sign.

Officials were also finding that the best code breaker was a "mature and dependable" person with a "clear, bright mind"—but someone "young enough to be alert, adaptable, able to make adjustments readily, willing to take supervision," and "able to withstand inconveniences of Washington." This description fit many schoolteachers, including Dot Braden, to a T.

There was another reason schoolteachers like Dot were perfect. They were almost always unmarried. In America in the 1940s, three-quarters of local school boards (like other employers of female labor) required that married women not be hired and that a teacher resign when she did marry. Married women tended to move to follow their husbands. And at the time, many people believed that a wife's place was in the home.

Schoolteachers were smart, educated, accustomed to hard work, used to low pay, and youthful and mature at the same time. They were the perfect workers.

At Arlington Hall there were no unimportant jobs, but some tasks were harder than others.

Dot was put to work sorting messages, a common first

assignment. After a couple of days spent untangling messages that had been intercepted from American listening posts around the world, Dot showed she was capable of recognizing the numbers at the beginning of a message. These let the code breakers know the station from which the message had been sent.

Next she was presented with a series of four-digit numbers and told to detect any pattern she might see. A girl beside Dot started crying, but Dot faced the numbers in front of her with a reasonable amount of confidence.

Dot did not find the work easy. It felt like a complicated puzzle. But she must have done all right. She was told that she was being moved on to the next level.

Over the next few weeks Dot sat through lectures on the basics of code breaking and code making. She learned a bit about codes used by the Japanese Army. She absorbed the principles of how the Japanese Army was organized and the basics of the Japanese language used in military communications. She watched movies that aimed to inspire patriotism and build morale. Most of all, she sat through still more talks on the importance of security, secrecy, and silence. She was terrified she would accidentally bring a piece of paper home or let the wrong word slip. She constantly monitored her own behavior, even when she was not working at the compound.

Dot also was called for a one-on-one interview. The interviewer, a woman, asked her what languages she knew; what science and math courses she had taken; when she had graduated from high school and when from college. She was asked whether she had worked with radios and whether she liked the physics classes she had taken in college. The interviewer wanted to know what her hobbies were. "Books and bridge," Dot answered. The interviewer wrote that she was "attractive and well-dressed" as well as "intelligent" and "nice."

Based on this, her assignment was made, and it consisted of one word: crypt.

Dot had been assigned to one of the most urgent missions in Arlington Hall: breaking the codes that were being used to direct Japanese merchant ships around distant Pacific islands. The ships were bringing vital supplies to Japanese Army troops. Dot would be cracking the messages that controlled—and foretold—their movements. Cutting off the enemy's lifeline of food, fuel, and other critical supplies would allow the United States to push back against the Japanese in the Pacific Ocean. Tens of thousands of American men's lives were at stake.

Dot Braden would be sinking Japanese ships.

Dot Braden (right) and Ruth "Crow" Weston (left).

CHAPTER FIFTEEN

"I'm Saving It!"

December 1943

Dot Braden hated living at Arlington Farms. The dormitory walls were so thin that they shook when a person walked down the hall. The women always had to stand in line for something—the mailboxes, the showers, the cafeteria food, the phone, the bus. Local residents had opened their homes to the new government girls, called g-girls, and Arlington Hall was getting up and running, but there still wasn't enough housing for the women flooding into Washington.

Developers began building apartment buildings around Arlington Hall. One day Dot's friend Liz pointed out an ad for a new complex called Fillmore Gardens. Liz suggested they move in together, and they asked another colleague, Ruth Weston, if she wanted to go in with them. Ruth also lived in Idaho Hall and had gone through the same orientation classes as Dot. The two young women chatted on the bus back and forth to work.

Ruth Weston agreed that it would be nice to get away from the crowded dorm. The Fillmore Gardens apartment had a single bedroom, a single bathroom, a kitchen, and a living room. The apartment complex was not yet finished, but the place seemed like a palace—and well constructed— compared to Arlington Farms. The women could cook and eat when and where they wanted to and would have to share their bathroom only with one another. Their new place was a mile and a half from Arlington Hall, so they could walk to work rather than waiting for the bus.

Finding furniture was not easy. Materials were scarce, as were funds. Dot's mother sent a bed frame on the train from Lynchburg. The women decided that Liz would sleep on a cot and Dot and Ruth would sleep in the bed together. The problem was that the bed lacked a mattress. So Dot and Ruth found a store that sold mattresses and took the bus and streetcar downtown after work. They paid for the mattress and then realized the store didn't deliver. Dot went inside and found a salesman who looked as though he might be closing up for the day.

"We've got this mattress and we don't have any way to get it home," Dot told the man. "We live in Arlington. You all didn't deliver it."

"We weren't supposed to deliver it," the salesman told her. Then he relented. "Well, I'll tell you what—I live in Arlington and I'm going home. I can put the mattress on the top of my car. If you, where you live, have got some eggs, I've got a pound of butter with me. You all can cook me some eggs and use my pound of butter and I'll take your mattress for you."

So that's what they did. They traded a plate of scrambled eggs for the delivery of a mattress. The women weren't worried about having a strange salesman in their small apartment. With three women in the place they figured they could take care of themselves.

The mattress escapade was the beginning of Dot Braden's great friendship with Ruth Weston.

Ruth Weston was always willing to go along with the adventures Dot suggested. Whether it was letting a strange man deliver a mattress to their home, or traveling all the way to the beach and back during their one day off, Ruth Weston was game.

Ruth had grown up in the crossroads of Bourbon, Mississippi, where she was one of seven children. Bourbon was surrounded by cotton plantations. Ruth's father served as postmaster and owned a general store. He also farmed, but not well. The Depression was hard on the Weston family. The children worked in the store, and if they sold five dollars' worth of items between opening and closing, that was a big day. In June 1931 their father suffered a stroke.

Ruth's mother was open about the fact that she didn't want girls. But education was important, even for her three daughters. Ruth's maternal grandparents came from Germany and saw higher education as a way for the family to become Americanized. Ruth had an older sister, Louise, and a younger sister, Kitty, and all three of them went to Mississippi State College for Women. The Weston girls all majored in math.

Before the war, Ruth had struggled to find a teaching job. When she did find one, in a place called Pleasant Grove, she taught at a school with no heat, electricity, or running water for just $71 a month (roughly $1,000 today). She lasted one year, then found a job in Webb, Mississippi, which was also low paying, but a little less primitive.

Once the war started, the Weston family's German roots became problematic. People would ask Ruth's brothers whose side their mother was on. Their mother felt proud of her German heritage, but the whole family were loyal, patriotic Americans. Ruth's father flew an American flag every day. People in the area looked up to him as a leader even after he had his stroke. Ruth was close to him.

She shared his patriotism and commitment to public service. The Arlington Hall job was perfect for her.

In addition to her math skills, Ruth Weston was a talented piano player. But what Ruth was most famous for was this: You could tell her anything and she'd keep it to herself. She was the most closemouthed person imaginable. Her shyness made teaching hard. Ruth called teaching a "respectable way of starving to death," but also she disliked being the center of attention.

The family was never quite sure how Ruth had found out about the job at Arlington Hall. Her brother Clyde was surprised when investigators called to ask about his sister's background. In the chaos of many brothers shipping out to military service, Ruth managed to slip away without attracting as much notice as the boys did, making the two-day train ride from nearby Leland, Mississippi, to Washington.

Apart from her skill at keeping secrets, the other good thing about Ruth Weston was that you could tell her anything and she would not judge. For Dot, this was a relief from the snobbery of old-line Virginians, and even among her own family. The two young women confided in each other as they lay in their shared bed.

Yet certain things they did not share. Close as they were, Dot and Ruth confided nothing to each other about their work, even though they sometimes had lunch together in the Arlington Hall cafeteria and were, in fact, working on different areas of the same Japanese Army code-breaking effort. They went around terrified that they would let something slip. "We were scared to death," as Dot put it.

―――――――――――――――

Ruth's full name was Carolyn Ruth Weston. Sometimes she went by Ruth, sometimes by Carolyn. One day the milkman delivered the bill to the new Arlington apartment and addressed it to "Crolyn." Dot thought the misspelling was the funniest thing she had ever seen. She started calling Ruth "Cro-lyn," and over time the nickname shortened into "Crow." The name stuck: Crow. At least, that's what Dot called her. Nobody else did. It was like a secret code name.

The apartment soon became more crowded. Crow's older sister, Louise, wrote them saying she, too, wanted to come to Washington to look for government work. Crow was not happy to hear this. She had been glad to get out from under the thumb of Louise, known in the family as Sister. But what could she do? Crow and Dot went to fetch Sister from Union Station.

They showed Sister how to navigate the bus and the

streetcar and took her back to Fillmore Gardens, where she would sleep in the living room on a daybed. (Liz had a cot in the bedroom.) There were advantages to the Mississippi influx. Sister would make red beans and rice. Dot had never eaten Cajun food, and it was a treat on a cold day after finishing an eight-hour shift and walking a mile and a half home in the rain.

The women paid their own bills and cooked their own food. At any given time there might be five or even six women in the one-bedroom apartment. Sister stayed; Crow's little sister, Kitty Weston, came up for the summer. Dot's mother often took the bus up for visits, as did friends and family members from home. Crow's brother Clyde was stationed with the Navy in New York and came down to see them. He would flirt with Dot, who he thought was "a real cute girl" and a good friend to Crow.

Having all those people in one small place did not seem hard. They ate Sister's red beans and rice, and frozen peaches, which was the kind of thing you had for dessert when you couldn't get sugar. They would laugh about how their mouths froze and puckered from the peaches, and they would sit around the apartment talking with frozen lips.

Liz's mother visited from North Carolina and made green beans using fatback, fat from the back of a pig.

Liz's mother then fished the fatback out of the beans and wrapped it up to use again. "I'm saving it," she explained. That seemed very country to Dot and Crow, and "I'm saving it" became a mutual joke. "I'm saving it!" they would say, and fall over laughing.

Dot and Crow got along perfectly in every way.

During their off hours, many women wrote letters to soldiers and sailors.

CHAPTER SIXTEEN

So Many Girls

At Arlington Hall, the presence of so many code-breaking girls from small towns presented a challenge to their bosses. The top brass felt the women needed educating. Speakers were invited to teach the young women about geography and to stress how important their jobs were.

One of the first dignitaries to address the young women was Rear Admiral Joseph R. Redman, director of Naval Communications. His brother, John, was also a naval communications officer and headed up the code-breaking unit. In his lecture, "The Navy Attacks," Joseph Redman tried to give them an idea of the sheer enormousness of the Pacific Ocean. Newspaper reports gave the impression that ships from opposing navies were always just somehow finding each other, when really the task of finding an enemy ship was a bit like finding a needle in a haystack.

Naval battles only took place, Redman said, because of

the work of code breakers who could help pinpoint enemy movements. "The work you are doing—as dull as it may seem to you—is very exciting to someone else, and the information you are able to fire [to] the operating agencies in the field contributes a great deal to that success," he told the women. "And some days when it is hot, and you feel tired and sleepy, remember that the delay of a few hours in picking up some important information may have a vital bearing upon the operations that are going on out in the ocean."

The speakers were all high-level. Perhaps most thrilling was a talk revealing the inner workings of the Federal Bureau of Investigation, whose assistant director, Hugh H. Clegg, came to deliver a lecture called "The Enemy in Our Midst." Clegg talked about the FBI's own war—against criminals, informers, kidnappers, spies, and anyone who supported America's enemies. His remarks contained a joke that shows just how ferociously the agencies were competing for female workers. "Immediately upon arrival, I was threatened," he remarked. "Threatened that if I undertook in any way to try to recruit any of the lovely young ladies of this audience to come down and work in our fingerprint identification bureau, that there would be another casualty of war hobbling back in the general direction of Washington."

But even as the Arlington women were being educated and courted, they were receiving a subtle message that their involvement in the war effort—these apartments they were renting together, the furniture they were buying, the meals they were cooking, their newfound independence—was creating troubling social changes. A talk by Charles Taft, titled "America at War," centered on this idea. Taft, son of the late president William Howard Taft, served as director of the Office of Community War Services, a new agency created to cope with the disruptions of the Second World War on the home front.

Taft talked about the fact that factories and construction projects were drawing workers to communities that were hardly able to hold them. Minority groups were moving to find higher-paying work in places that had never seen them before. New industries were setting up overnight in communities without the schools, housing, playgrounds, and hospitals the workers would need.

But the main problem Taft saw was the women themselves. Taft saw a society that was being harmed by the fact that women had left the home for the public world. Women and their newfound freedoms, he believed, threatened society.

It was true that these newfound freedoms were changing the women's lives. Men, now, were the ones eager to get married. Men were the ones who wanted to have someone back home to write to, someone waiting when they came back from war, wounded or whole. Women—often—were the ones holding out for a bit more time to think. Dot Braden herself was in a bit of a pickle in that department.

At the time, the only real way for men and women to stay in touch was to write letters. Long-distance phone calls were expensive and soldiers often didn't have access to a phone, nor did women living in dorms or boarding-houses. At Fillmore Gardens, there was one telephone in the basement. But everybody had stationery and pen and pencil, and everybody, everywhere, was writing letters. The censorship department read the letters to make sure secret locations were not revealed, but that didn't stop the letters from traveling back and forth across thousands of miles of land and ocean.

Dot, for her part, had no fewer than five men she was writing to. Two were her brothers. The third was her sup-posed fiancé, George Rush, a tall young man whom she had dated at college. George had been a good college boy-friend. He was an enthusiastic dancer and liked going to mixers.

Dot and George had not seen each other much in the

past year, however. He entered the Army in April 1942 and kept getting moved farther west. He was stationed in California and had sent Dot a diamond engagement ring. Dot liked George but never envisioned spending her life with him. She wanted to send the ring back, but young women were told not to upset soldiers who were away from home, so she kept it. But she never really thought of herself as engaged. At one point, George had made the cross-country train ride back to Lynchburg and showed up on Dot's doorstep. He wanted Dot to marry him and move to California to be near him, but she refused.

Dot had also begun exchanging letters with Jim Bruce, an Army meteorologist whose family owned a dairy farm in Rice, Virginia. She had known him for several years. For quite some time, Jim had been after her to take off George Rush's ring. There was something steady about Jim. He was in meteorological training for the Army at the University of Michigan, and from time to time he would come to Lynchburg and look Dot up.

At one point Jim said, "I bet you're going to marry me." Dot put him off. But she always had Jim Bruce in the back of her mind. He did look spiffy in his uniform.

There was another soldier she was writing to. Dot had met Curtis Paris at a Washington dance. Curtis was a fellow southerner and had asked if he could write to her.

This was a common request—men were always asking to write—and Dot didn't see any reason to say no.

Dot didn't take it seriously. All the girls were writing letters, often to lots of soldiers. One was writing to twelve different men. It was fun and it felt like they were helping the war by keeping up morale. The women sent snapshots: small black-and-white pictures showing them in front of the US Capitol, or sunbathing, with a handwritten message on the back.

Soldiers and officers also streamed in and out of Washington, and it was possible for a woman to have a different date for every meal of the day. But it wasn't just women who were dating more than one person. One day Dot got a phone call from Jim Bruce, who was being sent overseas and wanted Dot to come down to see him off. "I'll have to let you know," she told him, in some confusion.

When Dot called Jim back, the operator said, "I have another person calling Lieutenant Bruce. I let her go first. If you don't mind waiting I'll put you through afterward."

"You certainly are popular," Dot said when she was put through.

"That was my sister," Jim Bruce told her.

Dot wasn't fooled. There was another girl in the picture. "Well, I'm sorry, I can't go," she told him tartly.

The next morning there was a message tacked to the

door to her room at Arlington Farms. It said, "Lieutenant Bruce is coming to Washington this afternoon." She read the note and went on to work thinking she'd see him at the end of her shift, but while she was working, an administrator came to say she had a phone call. Security was so tight at Arlington Hall that it was hard for an outsider to get a call through, so Dot knew it must be urgent. The call was from one of Jim Bruce's sisters.

"Have you seen Jim?" his sister asked breathlessly. Jim was being shipped out sooner than he thought. Orders were often changed at the last minute to keep the enemy from anticipating troop movements. "I have talked to every girl he knows, and you were last on the list," his sister told Dot.

Jim showed up at the end of Dot's shift, unaware that his unit was trying to reach him. "You've got to be back at the boat," Dot told him. They said a quick good-bye, and that was the last time Dot Braden saw Jim Bruce for almost two years.

Life was like that. Men came and went. At night, air raid sirens would sometimes go off, signaling residents to turn off their lights and pull down their blackout shades. This happened when Dot and Crow were having dinner with an old friend of Dot's, Bill Randolph, who held a diplomatic post. Bill's mother lived in Alexandria, nearby. The sirens started wailing, so Bill pulled out his guitar and they all sat on the porch in the darkness, Dot and Crow and Bill and his mother, and sang into the night. Life was strange now, and often oddly pleasant, even as Dot kept big framed photographs of her brothers, Teedy and Bubba, and George Rush and Jim Bruce and worried about all of the men in her life, all the time.

Wartime Sorrow

Many of the code breakers suffered personal losses. Fran Steen lost a fiancé, shot down in the Pacific, early on. Many American men who had been stationed on Pacific islands before the attack on Pearl Harbor were now prisoners of war. Erma Hughes, a psychology major recruited out of the University of Maryland—her father, a bricklayer, sold land to finance her tuition—was sending care packages to classmates in POW camps. The ROTC students in her class had mostly become paratroopers. Erma could never be certain her care packages arrived and did not even know whether the intended recipients were alive, but she kept sending them just in case.

The loss of friends, classmates, brothers, and boyfriends was difficult and frightening. It made the women that much more aware of the importance of their work and the cost of failure.

CHAPTER SEVENTEEN

Operation Vengeance

April 1943

The Navy women broke and rebroke the Japanese fleet code that Agnes Meyer Driscoll had laid the groundwork for. They broke the inter-island ciphers, and they helped keep track of the movements of the Imperial Japanese Navy. Men in the Pacific would get well-deserved credit for famous victories like Midway, but most Pacific achievements were group ones. And the groups were made up of women.

Women outnumbered men in almost every unit of the Naval Annex. Though they did not receive public credit, some women did become legendary in the small sealed rooms where they were working. One enlisted member of the WAVES "had such a knack for running additives across unplaced messages and recognizing valid hits that for over a year she was allowed to do almost nothing else," one internal memo noted.

Many women dearly wanted to replace the men working overseas, but the Navy would not allow it. Fran Steen, from Goucher, wanted to fly airplanes. She asked the Navy to send her to flight school, but her request was denied. So she took her ground exam at Washington National Airport and learned to fly planes on her own.

As the women proved how good they were at their jobs, the few remaining male officers at the Annex had to figure out what else the women could and could not do. One male officer asked if women could be taught to shoot. Many code rooms at the Annex had pistols ready in the event of unwanted visitors, and pistols were worn by officers escorting "burn bags"—sacks in which all discarded papers were put—to the incinerator. Someone pointed out that some other bureau was letting its women shoot, so a decision was made. Fran Steen learned to shoot on the pistol range, as did Suzanne Harpole and Ann White.

It was hard, harrowing work—all of it—and the women took it seriously. Local institutions did what they could to honor the Navy women. There were ten thousand

WAVES working in the Washington area. Jelleff's department store had a fashion show in which WAVES served as models. They enjoyed free entry almost everywhere. In their downtime they could visit the National Zoo and the Washington Monument. The Capitol Theatre had piano playing and singalongs. The National Gallery had musicians in its rotunda. The Washington Opera gave free performances on a barge on the Potomac River. The women sat on the steps near the river or rented canoes and paddled over, resting their oars in the mud while they listened. The Marine Band played behind the US Capitol; the National Symphony played in Constitution Hall.

There were splendid hotels in Washington: the Willard, the Carlton, the Statler, the Mayflower. Most held dances with big bands and lots of swing dancing. The women would go to American University and watch the Navy men playing baseball. They would sail on Chesapeake Bay. Theaters were open all night. You could go to a movie anytime. You never knew whom you would see. One WAVES member went to dinner with a lieutenant and found herself chatting with US general Dwight D. Eisenhower and his wife. Another met President Roosevelt himself at a party for disabled veterans.

A group of WAVES officers lived in a house where there were seven women and six beds. The women hot-bedded it, taking whatever bed was open. They would leave notes for one another on the pillows, sharing tips about hotels and restaurants that were giving away things free or had good discounts.

And they traveled. They could go anywhere on a train for a discounted fare. If they had a thirty-six-hour leave, the women would go to New York City. If they had seventy-two hours, they'd go farther. Ida Mae Olson invited her friend Mary Lou to visit her family in Colorado. Mary Lou had joined the WAVES because her parents had been killed in a car accident and her wealthy uncle had not known what to do with her. Mary Lou was terrified when she saw a group of Native Americans and asked Ida Mae if they would attack.

Even just in the rooming houses, people of all backgrounds were thrown together. The women's freedom brought other surprises, though, about the uglier side of their own country. Washington was in many ways a southern city. Whites and blacks did not attend the same public schools, and black residents lived in the poorest parts of the city. Virginia was worse. Northerners were shocked by the strict racial divisions. When Marjorie Faeder boarded a train to Virginia Beach to take a quick honeymoon with her new husband, the couple sat down in a deserted car with plenty of seats. They were told they were in the

"colored" car—they had not known such a thing existed—
and shooed into the whites-only car. Nancy Dobson was
horrified every time she took a bus from Washington into
Virginia. When the bus arrived in the middle of the bridge,
all the African American passengers had to get up and
move to the back, and there was "just this deadly hush."
Frances Lynd, from Bryn Mawr, needed to buy some furniture, so she hired two African American men with a
pickup truck to take her downtown to get it. When she
jumped in the cab with them—being from Philadelphia,
she thought nothing of it—the men were fearful to be seen
with a white woman sitting next to them.

As hard as the women worked, there were lighthearted
moments even in the code rooms. One night Jane Case's
unit got word that an admiral was coming to visit, and
they needed to have their unit spotless by the next day. It
was Jane's job to operate the floor-buffing machine, which
seemed nearly as big as a baby elephant, and harder to handle. She flipped the "on" switch and nothing happened.
She crawled underneath a table to plug the machine in and
backed out to see it flying all over the office. By the time
she wrestled it into submission, the place was a disaster.
They had to spend the whole night picking up messages

before they could get the room painted and cleaned and buffed.

Jane had always been taught that a woman must be properly introduced to a man before going out with him, so for the entirety of the war she did not date. "When I think of it—I could have gone out with a lot of people," she said, regretfully, later. "The rules were so set, all my life."

For many other women, their social lives were as exhausting as the code-breaking work itself. Edith Reynolds, from Vassar, found herself courted by an Irish major who at one point had been in charge of mules for the British Army. There was another suitor she wasn't wild about who flew his mother from Seattle to meet her. Edith realized, with shock, that he thought they were going to get married. She broke up with him and he married her roommate instead.

One code breaker was standing in a movie line and realized there was a naval officer behind her. She turned to salute him, and he was so charmed by how flustered she was that they exchanged addresses and later married. At the group house where Edith Reynolds was living, they had a party and she noticed a man expertly cracking eggs into the eggnog. He was the plumber. "I came to fix a pipe, but this looked like so much fun, I stayed," he told her.

The women tended to ignore the Navy rule that forbade socializing between officers and enlisted persons. At the boardinghouse where Suzanne Harpole was living, there was an enlisted woman named Roberta. Suzanne and Roberta worked in the same office doing the same thing, and it seemed to them ridiculous not to be friends. Also boarding there were two women employed at Arlington Hall, and the four would use their free time to take trips to Williamsburg, Luray Caverns, and New York. The two Naval Annex women and the two Arlington Hall women could not talk about what they did, of course. They remained unaware of something even more interesting than the sights they saw: They were all breaking codes.

For the most part, the Navy and Army code breakers did not interact, or not knowingly. They likely ran into one another at all sorts of places—restaurants, movie theaters, streetcars—without realizing they were working on the same project. How could they? The work was top secret, and they couldn't talk about it.

Top officials at both code-breaking complexes did communicate, however. The Naval Annex had formal weekly meetings with Arlington Hall, and it was a WAVES officer, Ensign Janet Burchell, who crossed the river to serve as

Navy liaison for these meetings. The position required her to know about the code and cipher systems both operations were working. Ensign Burchell attended meetings where the two services discussed the forwarding of intercepts and captured materials; duplicate messages sent in different systems; reports of POW interrogations that might contain material useful to both; and other matters.

The Navy women had just missed taking part in the code-breaking triumph at Midway, but ten months later they were actively engaged in the other great code-breaking event of the Pacific naval war. On April 13, 1943, a message came through in JN-25. The code breakers weren't able to recover the whole message right away, but the fragments they did recover suggested that the commander in chief of the Japanese fleet—Admiral Yamamoto himself—was headed to Ballale (now Balalae) Island on April 18.

The initial break was made in the Pacific, but Washington also got busy, recovering additives and code groups so that blanks could be filled in. More messages were intercepted, and the fast-working, far-flung teams exchanged findings. Among those digging out code recoveries was Fran Steen from Goucher. The inter-island cipher JN-20 carried more details about Yamamoto's upcoming trip, adding facts and insights. Together the code breakers were able to reconstruct Yamamoto's precise schedule, which called for a day of hops between Japanese bases in the Solomon Islands and New Britain.

It was an extraordinary moment. The Americans knew exactly where the enemy's most valuable—and irreplaceable—naval commander would be, and when. Yamamoto was known for punctuality. Nimitz and other top US war officials decided Yamamoto would be shot down. It was not a light decision, assassinating an enemy commander, but they made it.

In what was known as Operation Vengeance, sixteen US Army fighter planes went into the air on April 18, taking off from a Guadalcanal airfield. They knew Yamamoto would be flying in a Japanese bomber the Americans called a Betty, escorted by fighter planes. The Americans calculated their own flight plan to meet Yamamoto over Bougainville. They flew for so long that the pilots were getting drowsy; the white coastline of Bougainville was racing beneath them when one of the pilots broke radio silence and shouted, "Bogeys! Eleven o'clock!" There was a hectic battle in which it never became clear who had shot down whom, but one Betty bomber plummeted into the trees, the other into the surf. Yamamoto's body was found in the Bougainville jungle, his white-gloved hand clutching his sword.

Cheering broke out at the Naval Annex when they heard the news. The architect of the Pearl Harbor attack was dead. The payback felt complete.

"Let me tell you, the day his plane went down, there was a big hoop-de-doo," recalled Myrtle Otto, the Boston-bred code breaker who had beat her own brothers in the race to enlist. "We really felt we had done something really fantastic, because that was—well, it was more than the beginning of the end. They knew it was coming down, but it was really—that was an exciting day."

A group of members of the WAVES on the way to Sugar
Camp.

CHAPTER EIGHTEEN

Sugar Camp

April 1943

They boarded the train at midnight, leaving Washington under sealed orders. The Navy women knew only that they were headed "west." The train was dirty and crowded. When it arrived at their destination, the women learned that "west" meant Dayton, Ohio.

Although this was a secret mission, a photographer stood waiting to greet them. The women lined up and smiled for group photos, smart and polished despite the all-night train ride. They wore their naval uniforms, of course.

A bus carried them from downtown Dayton into the nearby countryside. Soon they entered a peaceful, grassy compound called Sugar Camp, named after the maple trees that had once been tapped for syrup. There were rustic cabins clustered around a central clearing.

A Navy color guard greeted the women. The American

flag was raised. They lined up to receive linens and pillows and went to find their cabins. As fresh Navy recruits, their lives for the past two months had been a series of unfamiliar lodgings, first at boot camp and then in Washington, DC, where they spent several weeks taking tests, listening to security lectures, and waiting while their backgrounds were investigated. Nobody knew what kind of work they had been brought to Dayton to perform.

The small cabins were divided into two bedrooms, with two beds per room. Between the bedrooms was a bathroom. Soon—as more recruits began arriving, throughout April and into May—cots sometimes had to be squeezed in, to make room for an extra person.

Dayton had seen more than its fair share of inventors and entrepreneurs, including Orville and Wilbur Wright, the aviation pioneers. The mainstay of the city's economy was the National Cash Register Company, which owned Sugar Camp. NCR made the machines that kept American business running—accounting machines, adding machines, and cash registers.

But businesses' needs weren't as vital as the military's. NCR's ninety-acre industrial campus had been converted to producing the machinery of war. Around the country, major companies like Ford, IBM, Kodak, Bethlehem Steel, Martin Aircraft, and General Motors were all cooperating with the war effort. So were universities like Harvard and the Massachusetts Institute of Technology (MIT). One hundred percent of NCR's operations were now war-related work.

The women worked seven days a week, twenty-four hours a day, in shifts. Three times a day, more than a hundred of them would line up at Sugar Camp and march four abreast into Dayton, up hills and down, in snow and rain and sunshine, passing a house where a girl they called Little Julie would come to her window and wave at them. Before long, people in Dayton were saying you could set your clock by the sight of the WAVES marching. Their destination was the NCR main campus, located about a mile from Sugar Camp. A cover story explained their presence. "The WAVES will take courses in the operation of special accounting machines," announced the NCR newsletter.

The NCR complex in downtown Dayton occupied an area the size of eleven city blocks. The women worked in Building 26, a modest structure tucked away from the rest. Armed Marine guards patrolled the building. The women were locked inside the rooms where they worked.

They sat at big tables in rooms that each held about a dozen people. Hanging from a cord that plugged into the ceiling, or nestled in a little dish on the worktable before each of them, was a tool called a soldering iron. On the table in front of each woman was a wheel made of plastic, brass, and copper. The women were taught to use a soldering iron to fashion a little interlacing basket of wires that attached to each wheel. The wires were short and of varying colors. The women fashioned the wires according to diagrams, wrapping each wire around a prong and putting a dab of solder where the tip of the wire connected to the contact point of the wheel. Each woman would take the hot soldering iron and melt the solder. When it cooled, she would tug the wire to make sure the seal held. There was no room for mistakes.

It took a while to become expert—some never did and were given easier jobs—but most of the women were good with their hands.

Many of them already were familiar with machinery. Quite a few had worked as telephone operators before the war. Like Ronnie Mackey. She had grown up in Wilmington, Delaware. Another, Millie Weatherly, a North Carolinian, had been working alone on the Sunday of the Pearl Harbor attack. Her switchboard lit up as soldiers from a nearby base called home, some of them crying, to tell their parents they would not be home for Christmas. Millie connected their calls as fast as she could. About a year later her mother remarked, "You know, the Navy is welcoming women of good character and high school education." And so here Millie was, in Ohio.

Jimmie Lee Hutchison was just nineteen when she was working at Southwestern Bell in McAlester, Oklahoma. Jimmie Lee had four brothers in the service, and her fiancé, Robert Powers, was a pilot with the Army Air Force. The Navy sent a recruiter to the Southwestern Bell office where Jimmie Lee and her friend Beatrice Hughart were working. The two friends liked the idea of helping to bring the boys home. By the end of the day both had enlisted, Jimmie Lee by lying about her age.

At Hunter College, where Jimmie Lee took her naval aptitude test, she was surprised to learn she had a knack for reading blueprints. She had never seen one before, but something about the diagrams made sense. Her good friend Bea also got orders to Dayton, so here they were, working together, once again.

During rest periods, the women would put their heads down on the worktable, and the officer in charge, a former schoolteacher named Dot Firor, would read aloud from stories like *Little Women* and give them twenty minutes to let their minds drift. On the graveyard shift, some would sing to stay awake as they soldered.

The women were not told what the wheels they were wiring would be used for. They figured the wheels would be attached to some kind of machine, but what that machine did, they had no idea. There were men working one floor above them, constructing a machine the likes of which had never been seen, but the women didn't know that. They did know this: Whatever the wheels did, it must be important.

Circulating among them was a man named Joseph Desch, a Dayton inventor who was deeply involved in the secret project. Once the Sugar Camp cafeteria was up and running, Desch often would visit with the women at mealtimes along with his wife, Dorothy. Lieutenant Commander Ralph I. Meader, a Navy officer who lived with the Desches, was always at Joseph Desch's side.

But for much of the time, the women were left to their own devices. They worked hard, but—not having chores to do or houses to keep—enjoyed free time to read, write letters, and use the Olympic-size swimming pool on the grounds of Sugar Camp. In the early morning after finishing the graveyard shift, they would stroll back to camp, savoring the meadowlarks and the fresh smell of clover. One of the women, Betty Bemis, was a champion swimmer who had won several national titles, and men—Joe Desch, Ralph Meader, even Orville Wright—would come down to the pool to watch Betty practice.

The women were warned that when they went into Dayton, they should travel in pairs. It was fine for the women to date the soldiers and airmen who lived at nearby

Wright and Patterson airfields, but they were not to say anything about their work. Parts of the city were out of bounds. Many German Americans had settled in the southwestern part of Ohio. Most were loyal citizens, but there were remnants of the Bund, an organized group of Nazi sympathizers. The women were told they could be kidnapped and that German spies would very much like to know what was happening in Building 26.

The women did not ask questions. They tried not to speculate on what they were making. Even so, it was impossible, during the long hours with their diagrams and soldering irons, not to notice that there were twenty-six wires and that the wheels had twenty-six numbers on them.

Twenty-six, of course, was the number of letters in the alphabet.

For the Allies, 1942 had marked the low point in the Battle of the Atlantic. In the last six months of that year, German U-boats sank nearly five hundred Allied ships as they tried to make the crossing between North America and England. Now 1943 was shaping up to be even worse. March 1943 had been the most terrible month of the whole war, with ninety-five Allied ships sunk by Nazi submarines.

The American war machine could not produce enough ships to make up for such heavy losses. The crisis was serious. England needed wheat and other food supplies. Joseph Stalin needed weapons to drive the Germans out of Russia. And the Allies needed to clear the Atlantic Ocean of the U-boat menace if they were ever to make the waters safe for the convoys that would be needed to transport troops and tanks and weapons in sufficient numbers to mount—at long last—an Allied invasion of France.

The British still had charge of code-breaking efforts in the Atlantic theater. But the Americans were becoming more than just a junior partner. It had taken a while for the two services to begin working together smoothly. The British Navy had been horrified by the amateurish nature of the US Navy's intelligence operation. The United States, in return, felt their English friends were withholding details about the Enigma project.

Both services were right, but an agreement was reached over time, and secure lines set up between American and British naval intelligence. Both services worked hard to track the U-boats and predict their movements. The effort was never easy, but it became excruciatingly difficult after February 1942, when the German subs started using a four-rotor naval Enigma instead of the three-rotor machine that had already been broken. Allied efforts against the new system, nicknamed Shark, proved mostly futile. During this dark period the Allies struggled to predict U-boat movements using other methods, including radio signals. But the impenetrability of the four-rotor Enigma kept them at a major disadvantage.

Finally, in late October 1942, four British destroyers patrolling the eastern Mediterranean attacked a U-boat. The submarine, which had surfaced, began to sink, and a group of British sailors tore off their clothes, dove into the water, and swam over to it to retrieve papers and equipment. Two of the sailors, an officer and a seaman, went down with the sub and with the German sailors. The others were able to scramble into a whaler with the information they had risked their lives to find. The men found a weather cipher book that helped the Bletchley Park code breakers get into the four-rotor Enigma cipher. They broke Shark for the first time using the bombe machine, to find a message showing the position of fifteen U-boats. They were back in.

Even with this assistance, though, the Allies' ability to break the Enigma ciphers was spotty. Cipher books changed, and often the Allied code breakers had to try to come up with the key using hand methods. The British bombe machines could not help. Because the extra, fourth rotor created twenty-six times more ways to encipher each letter, the older British bombes would have to run twenty-six times faster, or there would have to be twenty-six times more of them, to test every possibility.

What was needed, to attack the naval Enigma, was a much faster bombe. Allied officials decided that America would build scores, maybe even hundreds, of high-speed machines capable of handling the four-rotor Enigma cipher. The Navy hired Joseph Desch, the Dayton inventor, to design an American bombe. Desch had an engineer's genius, the ability to work with his hands, and real-life experience in how a factory floor functioned.

A plan was drawn up: Desch would design a high-speed bombe, working with Navy engineers and mathematicians. The machine would be built by Navy mechanics and NCR employees. The Navy women—though they did not know it—had been brought to Dayton to wire thousands of "commutator wheels" to go on the front of the American bombe machine, fast-spinning wheels to test possible settings.

In short: What the Americans were going to produce was a roomful of high-powered machines that the Germans thought could never be built.

On the grounds of Sugar Camp.

CHAPTER NINETEEN

Breaking Shark

Summer 1943

In Dayton, Building 26 was modified and renamed the US Naval Computing Machine Laboratory. Its purpose was to build faster bombe machines to recover the key settings for the four-rotor Enigma machines. Meanwhile, the Naval Annex in Washington set up a top secret "research" group of engineers and mathematicians to work with inventor Joseph Desch.

A number of the research department's mathematical staff were female. Like everybody else, the Navy was eager to find women capable of doing higher math—the very field that women long had been discouraged from entering. The Naval Annex put out the word to boot-camp evaluators, asking them to be on the lookout for enlisted women who scored high on the math aptitude test. These women had not enjoyed anything like the same educational opportunities the men had. They did, however, have the smarts, the desire, and the ability. In the bombe project, many found the kind of work that they had been looking for all their lives.

One such woman was Louise Pearsall, a twenty-two-year-old from Elgin, Illinois. The oldest of four, Louise attended high school on scholarship at the private Elgin Academy. She went to the University of Iowa, where she was the only woman in many of her math classes—the chalk-covered calculus professor used to stare at her as he paced the room, flustered by her presence—and performed well. But she left after two years because her father struggled to afford the tuition and didn't think it would pay off with a job. Louise enlisted in the WAVES, expecting to be made an officer, but the first class of female officers filled so quickly that she went in as an ordinary seaman.

At a specialized training camp in Madison, Wisconsin, Louise took classes in physics, Morse code, and radio operation. She was held up from graduating because of an audio dyslexia that made it hard for her to master receiving Morse. Instead of becoming a radio operator, she was rerouted to the Enigma project. In March 1943 she got orders to travel to Washington, where, at the Naval Annex, she underwent more tests and interviews and found herself assigned to work for John Howard, a professor from MIT.

As the new high-speed bombes were being designed, it was Louise's job to sit at a desk and do what the bombe would ultimately do faster: test Enigma key settings. She worked on variations, figuring out, if X became M, and T became P, what was the mathematical formula that would take a letter through the right sequence. It was difficult and stressful work.

To come up with an Enigma key setting, the naval team had to understand more than math. They had to understand the nature of the messages that German U-boat commanders sent. Submarines constantly communicated with headquarters, providing updates that enabled German admiral Dönitz to make decisions and issue orders. Since the boats were often thousands of miles from Germany, messages were sent over high-frequency circuits that could cover long distances. This opened them up to enemy interception.

So the Allied mathematicians went about learning German naval greetings, the names of U-boats and commanders, and how German messages tended to be phrased. They knew a short message from Dönitz might include an order to "report your position" or to head for a port on the French coast. Subs often reported location and fuel capacity. All of this helped the code breakers come up with cribs. If they suspected that a line of cipher such as

RWIVTYRESXBFOGKUHQBAISE

represented the German phrase "weather forecast Biscay":

WETTERVORHERSAGEBISKAYA

they would line up the two lines of type, write numbers over or under them,

1 2 3 4 5 6 7 and so on

and look for "loops," places where one letter turned into another, and then that second letter turned into another. In the above example, they would see that *E* paired with *T* at position 5, *T* with *V* at 4, *V* with *R* at 7, *R* with *W* at 1, and *W* with *E* at 2, closing the loop. When the bombes were up and running, they would be able to program these loops into the bombe machine, which sought a setting where all these loops would happen. Since they didn't yet have machines, Louise herself and a tiny team of colleagues were the bombe, "working in an office on figures," as she later put it. "We had no equipment. We didn't have anything, really, to do anything big with. We were just getting started."

The Enigma had a few weaknesses that helped them. No letter could be enciphered to itself—that is, *B* would never become *B*. The machine had a reciprocal quality, meaning that if *D* became *B* on a certain key setting, then *B* became *D*. These factors limited the encipherments, but only somewhat; the possibilities still ran into the billions. Sometimes the team would get a key setting and be able to read messages for a couple of days. Other times all their efforts to find a key setting failed. There would be moments of clarity and long periods of darkness. The inconsistency of their work—and the helplessness when they could not recover a key setting—was dreadful. Ann White, from Wellesley, was working in the unit that translated broken Enigma messages from German to English. She always remembered one terrible night when a high-ranking naval officer came in, gave them a message, and begged, "Can't you give us any clues?"

She couldn't. She wondered how many lives would be lost because of that.

As the summer of 1943 approached, John Howard told Louise Pearsall she needed to learn how to shoot a pistol. Some members of the mathematical research unit were relocating to Dayton, and she was one of those picked to go. She began target practice with a .38. In early May she and four other women, with about the same number of men, got their guns, boarded the train, and headed west to Dayton. Soon they, too, found themselves billeted at Sugar

Camp. Unlike their bunkmates, these women knew why they were there.

They were going to help make the bombes work.

Joe Desch was working to perfect the first two experimental bombes, called Adam and Eve. He was under a lot of pressure. Commander Ralph Meader was always telling him to hurry up, that he'd be responsible for the deaths of countless more sailors and merchant seamen if he didn't come through with a high-speed bombe—and soon.

It wasn't just a matter of getting the math to work; it was a matter of getting the machinery to run. The bulky bombes, which stood seven feet tall and ten feet long and weighed more than two tons, had hundreds of moving parts, and even a bit of copper dust could foul the works. Some components did not exist and had to be designed and made. The staff in NCR's Electrical Research unit swelled from seventeen in August 1942 to eight hundred in May 1943, building the machines and perfecting the design.

In the Navy, a newly launched and commissioned warship makes a "shakedown cruise" to work out the kinks and get ship and crew running smoothly. The bombe's shakedown cruise started in May 1943, around the time Louise Pearsall arrived. It was her team's job to troubleshoot, together with Desch and Howard and some of the men who built the bombe. Many things could—and did—go wrong: "Encountered some incorrect wiring and shorting of the wheel segments by small copper particles" was one of many entries recording problems and mistakes.

The unit worked in a fever. Louise Pearsall's team would make up a menu, set the commutators, then start the bombe going. If the wheels produced a "hit," that meant the combination they'd entered into the machine might represent that day's key setting. They would test the hit on an M-9, a small machine that replicated an Enigma. The team would feed a message into M-9 and see if it produced German. If so, they had hit the jackpot: They had found the correct key setting.

Louise got one of the first jackpots. She came up with a menu that produced a hit, and when they sent the results to Washington, a colleague there called back and congratulated her. "You just cracked one," they told her. Her break provided evidence that the bombes could do what they were supposed to.

By June, the bombes were working, but fitfully. More machines were brought online and they repeatedly broke down.

Louise worked herself into exhaustion. On July 6 she was able to take a weeklong leave and go home to Elgin, where her father tried to get her to reveal what she was doing. She didn't crack. He lived the rest of his life without knowing that Louise had put his two years of college tuition payments to better use than he ever could have imagined.

———————

By September the team had put the finishing touches on the first generation of high-speed bombes. Over the summer the Navy had constructed a "laboratory building" in the Mount Vernon compound in Washington. It was time to put the bombes to work.

In Dayton, crates containing bombes were loaded onto flatbed train cars in the dark of night. Other bombes would follow, more than a hundred in all, in the coming weeks. NCR also built M-9s and shipped those as well. Louise Pearsall rode with one of the first shipments. The train was late leaving. Louise was sitting in her seat, wondering why they were delayed, when her boss, John Howard, sat down and confided that men had been detained. The Navy suspected they were going to sabotage the train either by making sure it wouldn't reach Washington or somehow stealing its top secret cargo.

Louise and Howard were the only ones who knew the reason for the delay. Louise Pearsall spent the long overnight trip back to Washington sitting bolt upright in her seat.

Courtesy of DC Department of Transportation

The US Navy's code-breaking operation at Mount Vernon Seminary.

CHAPTER TWENTY

The Tables Turn

September 1943

The crew in Washington worked overtime to get the bombes up and running. Several hundred of the women at Sugar Camp made the return trip east from Dayton to Washington, to live in Barracks D and run the bombe machines, though they still did not know the machines' true purpose.

Louise Pearsall, who did, continued troubleshooting. Though the DC bombe crew would soon consist of nearly seven hundred women, it started as a smaller group, and she worked seven days a week, twelve hours a day.

The bombe was a "high, high, high priority project," as Louise later put it, and everybody on it was important. Sloppy or tired work was not acceptable. Their work meant life or death for American men.

Just how important the women were became clear

when Louise's brother Burt, a hotshot Marine pilot, tried to get into the Naval Annex compound to visit her. Both of Louise's brothers were in the military, and both were big deals at home in Elgin. Not here. Here, Louise was the big deal. When Burt approached the first set of guards at the Naval Annex with a couple of pilot buddies, he informed the guards—fellow Marines—that they were going inside to see his sister. "No, you're not," the guards replied, barring their way. Louise had to come outside after her shift. They hired a cab and asked the driver to take them slowly down Constitution Avenue, and Louise showed her younger brother the Washington sights.

That visit was a rare break. The Enigma project took its toll on everybody connected with it. The people working on it were mathematicians and engineers. They were precise, conscientious people who liked to solve problems and build beautiful things, not kill people. The work was particularly hard on women like Louise who knew the stakes. A daily-log entry spoke of the "terrific pressure" everyone was under.

However they chose to relieve their stress, the women were unwilling to abandon their duties for long. Louise Pearsall was annoyed when, toward the end of 1943, she was told she could not remain in the ranks of the enlisted. Given her detailed knowledge of one of the war's most top secret projects, the Navy insisted she become an officer. In January 1944 she was sent to Smith College for officer training.

A newly minted naval officer is rarely sent back to the same place where he or she worked as an enlisted person, but Louise Pearsall was a special case. After two months at Smith she returned to the Naval Annex during the week ending March 18, 1944, wearing her ensign bars. A lieutenant working in personnel said John Howard had been driving them crazy, asking when Louise would get back. She was sitting in a routine orientation class when a lieutenant commander came in and told her to go on back to work. "Louise, would you get out of here right now?" he told her. "I'm tired of listening to your boss."

***

Everybody became experienced and good at their jobs pretty quickly. After just six months in the Navy, the young women who had wired the commutators—and now were running the bombes in Washington—found themselves supervising women even younger and greener than they were. Jimmie Lee Hutchison, the switchboard operator from Oklahoma, was in charge of a four-person bombe bay. Jimmie Lee's friend Beatrice worked a machine nearby. Their workplace took up the entire bottom floor of the laboratory building. It was an airplane hangar–like space with three rooms, each room divided into "bays" containing four machines. There were 120 bombe machines in all. The machines were noisy; on summer days the room got so hot that the women opened the windows to keep from passing out. When they did, the racket could be heard from outside on Nebraska Avenue.

As a bay supervisor, Jimmie Lee Hutchison had an assistant and four operators. When she came on duty, she signed a logbook that lay on top of a printer near the bombes. It was Jimmie Lee's job to keep the log, supervise the bay, and set up one of the machines according to a menu she was given.

Doing so meant moving the commutator wheels and rotating them to the starting position. The wheels were heavy—weighing nearly two pounds—and had to be carefully placed so they wouldn't fly off and break somebody's leg. She would set the wheels, sit on a stool, and wait to see if she got a hit. If she didn't, she'd have to move the wheels, rotate them again, and start over.

When the machines got a hit, they produced a printout of the setting that got the hit. Jimmie Lee would take the printout to a window where a gloved hand belonging to an unseen female officer would take it.

Some days, the wheels were changed over and over

and over again without getting a hit. It was tiring work that required energy and concentration. The women hated the long "hoppities," when they were testing a possible wheel turnover and had to get up and down, up and down, changing the wheels several times on the same run.

Jimmie Lee by now had married her high school sweetheart, Bob Powers. By a lucky coincidence, Bob had been assigned to ferry planes into the airfields at Dayton, bringing planes up from North Carolina and from Bowman Field in Kentucky. They married at Bowman Field on June 18, 1943. Back in Dayton, Jimmie Lee's WAVES friends threw them a party. After that, the newlyweds spent time together whenever Bob Powers flew into Dayton.

After Jimmie Lee was sent to Washington, though, their visits were few and far between.

As Jimmie Lee and the other women settled into their duties, they became part of an Enigma code-breaking chain that was virtually all female. When a message arrived at the Annex, it would first go to the cribbing station. The cribbers had one of the hardest jobs, sifting through intelligence from the war theater, including ship sinkings, U-boat sightings, weather messages, and battle outcomes. Scanning intercepts, they had to select a message that was not too long—a long message might involve more than one setting—and guess what it likely said. Comparing crib and message, they had to create a menu. Louise Pearsall did this; so did Fran Steen, the biology major from Goucher College. Fran had spent a year on the Japanese project, then moved to the German ciphers. Promoted to watch officer, Fran had access to a secure line that connected her to a counterpart in England. Her code name was "Pretty Weather."

From there, the menu would be passed to Jimmie Lee or another bombe deck operator. If there was a hit, it would go to somebody like Margaret Gilman, one of the women recruited in college, who would run it through the M-9 to see if the hit produced understandable German. Once they got a key setting, later messages for that day could be run through the M-9 and translated, without having to use the bombes.

Soon, the operation was so smooth that most keys were solved in hours and most messages decrypted immediately. The effect of the US bombes on solving the Atlantic U-boat cipher "exceeded all expectations," noted one internal Navy memo. "Since 13 September 1943, every message in that cipher has been read and since 1 April 1944 the average delay in 'breaking' the daily key has been about twelve hours. This means that for the last half of each day, we can read messages to and from Atlantic and Indian Ocean U-boats simultaneously with the enemy."

Once they were broken, the messages would pass to somebody like Janice Martin, who worked in the submarine tracking room, which was located one floor above the bombe deck. If anyone opened the door to the submarine tracking room, all they saw from the hallway was a blank wall. Inside, however, there was a huge map of the North Atlantic. The broken messages from the M-9 were sent up to Janice's office and translated. The U-boats had to report whether they sank an Allied ship or whether any U-boats had been sunk, and the women used these Enigma messages—along with files on individual U-boats and their commanders—to track, with pins, every U-boat and convoy whose location was known. At another desk, several other Goucher women tracked "neutral shipping," or ships that claimed not to be part of the war on either side, based on daily position reports. Neutral shipping mattered because if those ships deviated from their assigned sea-lanes, it might mean they were secretly supplying U-boats.

In addition to tracking the ships, researchers in Janice's room would put together an intelligence report overnight. Between seven thirty and eight a.m., there would be a knock on the door, and Janice's team would hand over an envelope containing the night's messages and the report. The messenger would put it in a locked pouch and take it to the Main Navy and Munitions Building downtown.

There, a commander named Kenneth Knowles, working with a counterpart tracking room in England, would make decisions about whether to use the intelligence to reroute convoys or to sink the U-boats. The downtown tracking room at first was staffed by enlisted men, but as the war continued, WAVES took over there as well. One male officer said the WAVES did a better job because they had had to meet stiffer selection requirements.

***

After the disasters of 1942 and early 1943, in which ship after Allied ship was sunk by U-boats, the Allies had a stunning turnaround in the Atlantic. By September 1943, most U-boats had been swept from the Atlantic waters. This was thanks not only to the new high-speed bombes but also to a host of other Allied war measures: advances in radar, sonar, and high-frequency direction finding; more aircraft carriers and long-range aircraft; better convoy systems. The Allies changed their convoy cipher, and Germany could no longer read it. The tables turned.

During the summer, American hunter-killer units used code breaking along with other intelligence to find and sink big German submarines that were sent out to refuel U-boats. These refuelers were known as milch cows, and between June and August, American carrier planes sank five. In October, they finished off all but one. The refuelers were critical to the U-boats' ability to stay so far away from their home base, and as the milch cows went down, the U-boats began to drift homeward.

There was always the chance, however, that the U-boats could come back. And they did try. In October 1943, the U-boats reappeared. But now the costs were punishingly high. For every Allied merchant vessel sunk, seven U-boats were lost. Now German admiral Dönitz was the one who could not build boats fast enough to replace those he was losing. In November, thirty U-boats ventured into the North Atlantic and sank nothing. The U-boats began lurking elsewhere, clustering around the coast of Britain. Dönitz was always trying to innovate the U-boats, adding a snorkel-like device called a *Schnorchel* that enabled them to remain submerged longer. He was willing to sacrifice his boats, and his men, to keep the U-boats in the water as a way to tie up Allied resources.

But it was a losing battle. The more U-boats the Germans made, the more the Allies sank. In May 1944 alone, the Allies sank half the U-boats in operation. More than three-quarters of the U-boat crews were killed, suffering terrible watery deaths. The women in the tracking room were aware of the full horror.

As 1943 gave way to 1944, the American bombes ran twenty-four hours a day. By now the British had handed over the four-rotor bombe operations entirely to the Americans.

And with the U-boats under control, Bletchley Park asked the Americans to help break the daily keys of the three-rotor Enigmas used by the German Army and Air Force. Louise Pearsall moved to the Air Force effort. The pace remained relentless as the European war thundered on. The women would spend the morning working naval U-boat ciphers and the rest of the day breaking the others.

The bombe machines would soon be called into heavy use, just prior to and during the invasion of France—D-Day.

The Hello Girls

World War II wasn't the first time switchboard operators were called upon to help defend their country. In World War I, the American, British, and French armies strung phone lines around Europe. They needed telephone operators to connect the calls. Switchboard operation was believed to be women's work, and male soldiers refused to do it.

French operators were not as skilled as American ones, so the Army Signal Corps recruited US switchboard operators who were bilingual in English and French and loaded them into ships bound for Europe.

Known as the "Hello Girls," these were the first American women other than nurses to be sent by the US military into harm's way. The officers whose calls they connected often prefaced their conversations by saying, "Thank Heaven you're here!"

The Hello Girls more than proved their expertise and courage. They remained at their posts even when ordered to evacuate during bombing in Paris, and they moved to the front lines to work the switchboards during explosions and fires.

CHAPTER TWENTY-ONE

Pencil-Pushing Mamas Sink Japanese Ships

March 1944

Ambon. Canton. Haiphong. Hankow. Kupang. Osaka. Palembang. Saigon. Wewak. Dot Braden had never heard of most of these places until a few months earlier. Now they kept her running from the big table where she worked, over to the overlappers' console, where messages encoded using the same additives were grouped together. Then Dot ran back again to her spot at the big table. These were the names of places, somewhere in Asia or the South Pacific, likely to be mentioned toward the beginning of messages coded in 2468, the main Japanese water-transport code.

The breaking of 2468—the water-transport code—had

created a need for thousands more workers to decode the stream of maru-related messages.

Transport code 2468 was everywhere. Anything anybody needed was sent by water. Water was how the rice was transported, and the soldiers, and the spare airplane parts. To move the goods the Japanese Army needed, the marus were always sailing. They sailed between Hiroshima, Yokohama, Wewak, Saipan, Tokyo, Manila, the Truk Lagoon. It was not necessary for Dot to know how to pronounce the cities and ports, but it was helpful to know the four-digit code groups that stood for them.

Code system 2468 filled Dot's brain.

Dot Braden was no longer explaining physics formulas to teenagers. Instead, she was sitting at a table puzzling over words she had never heard before she came to Arlington Hall. "Sono." "Indicator." "Discriminant." "GAT." The sono was the number added to messages that had been divided into parts before being transmitted. Sono #1 was the first part, Sono #2 was the second part, and so on. The discriminant was the number that identified the code system—for instance, 2468. The indicator was the tiny clue that told you what book to look in. GAT stood for "group as transmitted": the code group plus the cipher. The GATs were what you saw when you looked at the message for the first time.

Dot, of course, was not to utter any of these words outside the high wire double fences of the Arlington Hall compound. "This material is extremely secret and must be treated with the utmost care," one training document said. "Some of the words which you will consider elementary have been used only in this code, eg KAIBOTSU SU 'to sink a ship'. If you should mention this word to any one connected with the Axis or in some way succeed in letting it get into improper hands, this one fact alone would betray to the Japanese that we are reading their most recent transport code."

Dot never mentioned anything to anybody. She and Crow never discussed their work, even though they lived together, ate together, and shared a bed. When she wrote letters to her brothers, or to Jim Bruce or George Rush, she did not tell them what she did. She talked about eating red beans and rice and frozen peaches and going to the beach. She liked the work at Arlington Hall and had few complaints, apart from the fact that northerners thought southerners were less well educated and had funny accents.

At Arlington Hall, Dot was given cards with series of four-digit code groups plus a cipher, and it was her job to run the numbers against a bank of code groups she had memorized. The messages she got were the urgent ones—the ones that might require action. In other words, the ones that might tell the Navy where these valuable supply ships were headed—ships they could sink before they reached the enemy.

Dot would scan each one and compare the groups on the page to the code groups she kept stored in her head. She would look for a group whose position suggested that it likely meant "maru," or—this was always exciting— "embarking" or "debarking." Dot sat near a pole, and when she saw a code group that seemed important, she would jump up and almost hit her head on the pole as she ran to take the message to the overlappers' unit, a group of women who worked in another room. They would take her message and place it on a big piece of paper with other messages encoded using the same additives.

Often, a young woman named Miriam was the over-lapper waiting for Dot's handoff. Miriam was one of the most snobbish northerners Dot had ever known. One day, over lunch in the cafeteria, Miriam said, "I have never yet met a southerner who can speak proper English." This offended Dot, as it was intended to do. "Another smart-aleck New Yorker," she thought, but she did not say it.

Despite getting on each other's nerves, Dot and Miriam had to work seamlessly together, and they did. Dot would get the messages started by identifying some of the code groups, and Miriam would place the messages Dot brought her. From the overlapping station, the work sheet went to a reader, who would decipher the meaning. Information from the finished translations would make its way to the staff of General MacArthur or to a submarine captain who would do what needed to be done.

The language of the 2468 messages was short and no-nonsense. The messages consisted of sailing schedules, harbormaster reports, reports on the water levels of ports and transportation of cargo. Sailing schedules were the simplest. These included the transport number, the date, the time the maru would be arriving or leaving, and its destination. Others concerned the movement of troops or equipment. The marus carried everything: food, oil, supplies, and even human remains.

When a new message arrived, Dot looked for stereotypes, which were words that occurred frequently in the same place. "Maru" was a common one, but there were others as well, depending on the origin and the goods being transported. For example, one Singapore station transmitted a report of ships leaving for the island of Sumatra. Stereotypes might include the ship number or name, the date and hour of departure, the speed, the course, and the date and hour of scheduled arrival.

Another transmitted a daily weather report. Sitting at her table in Arlington, Virginia, Dot was amused at how many bits and pieces of information she knew about what the weather was like eight thousand miles away.

Here is how Dot did her work: Let's say she knew that the code group for "arriving" was 6286 and she knew where this word was likely to appear. She would find that place in the message and look at the four-digit code before her. Books at Arlington Hall listed common code words as well as possible enciphered versions. She would look for a match, or she could do the math in her head and strip out the additive herself. Sometimes—when they were desperate—the code breakers would take the code groups and encipher them with every possible additive. A smattering of 2468 code groups included:

4333 *hassoo*—to send things

4362 *jinin*—personnel

4400 *kaisi*—beginning, commencing

4277 *kookoo*—navigate, to sail

4237 *toochaku yotei*—scheduled to arrive

4273 *hatsu yotei*—scheduled to leave

Dot's workday consisted of messages that, once deciphered, said things like "PALAU DENDAI/ 2/ 43/ T.B./ TRANSPORT/ 918/ (/878/)/ 20th/ 18/ JI/ CHAKU/ ATESAKI/ DAVAO/ SEMPAKUTAI/ 4/ CEBU/ E.T./," outlining transport schedules between bases.

If it sounds hard and exhausting, it was. The Japanese Army's cryptologic system was highly complicated and changed often. That meant that Arlington Hall's Japanese Army code section had the hardest job in the place.

At Arlington Hall, a secret African American unit—mostly female, and unknown to many white workers—tackled commercial codes, keeping tabs on which companies were doing business with Axis companies.

CHAPTER TWENTY-TWO

One Sad Shoe

Spring 1944

Arlington Hall was a far cry from the Naval Annex when it came to attitude and culture. It was more of a civilian atmosphere. The Army's code-breaking operation was as serious as the Navy's when it came to work, but far more easygoing when it came to life.

For Dot Braden, "life" in Washington meant writing letters to men and having fun with other women. The same was true of her friend Crow, who was fun-loving but shy and didn't date much. Neither of them had much free time. Their schedule consisted of seven days of code-breaking work, followed by an eighth day off, followed by seven more days of work. On their one day off they'd be "dead dog tired," as Dot put it, but would have to do errands and grocery shopping.

They did have some adventures. Once, Dot had a friend

visiting from Lynchburg, and they decided to attend one of the hotel balls. As an icebreaker, the women were told to stand on one side of the dance floor and the men on the other. The women were instructed to throw one shoe onto the dance floor. The men were to pick up a random shoe and dance with whoever owned it. But the problem with shoes was this: People didn't have many, and they couldn't get new ones often. Shoes were rationed, and they had to save up ration coupons to buy a new pair. In the meanwhile, all anybody could do was get new soles for their existing shoes. With all the walking Dot did between her apartment and Arlington Hall—at least three miles each day—she was always wearing through the bottom of her shoes. For the dance she had worn one of her two good pairs, strappy white sandals. There was a hole as big as a quarter in the sole.

Dot lobbed the sandal onto the floor, and it flipped upside down in such a way that all the lights in the room seemed to be shining on that hole. No man grabbed it, and the shoe lay there, sad-looking, while couples danced around it. Dot didn't have a partner for that dance. She and her friend thought that was the funniest thing they'd ever seen, Dot's sad shoe upturned with that awful hole in it, and no man willing to pick it up.

Not being military, Dot and Crow couldn't take

the long train journeys the Navy women did. The military enjoyed discounts and seating priority. Dot and Crow would have to pay full fare and risk not getting a seat. Even so, the two friends managed to find plenty to occupy their rare free time. They went window-shopping downtown and perfected the art of looking dressy with very little money. They toured the museums and monuments and visited the National Cathedral, which was still under construction, but awe-inspiring even so. They took the local train up to Baltimore, which had nice stores, to buy hats. Back at the apartment, Crow's sister Louise—aka Sister—had a tendency toward gloominess. Dot decided to cheer her up by throwing a party for everybody living in Fillmore Gardens. Soon the young women were invited to other parties in the apartments of neighbors, who were mostly young couples.

On rare days off that weren't filled with errands, Dot and Crow sometimes took a succession of buses and streetcars to do a bit of sunbathing and swimming. A popular Chesapeake Bay day resort, Beverly Beach, offered a sandy beach area as well as a dance floor, bandstand, and slot machines. Colonial Beach, in Virginia, had a bathing area along the Potomac. Getting to either place took so long that it would nearly be time to come home by the time the women arrived, but they went anyway. The two code breakers would manage to get sunburned in what little time they had. When they got back they always suspected that Sister, who was fair and who wouldn't often risk going to the beach, was secretly glad to see them so red and sunburned. They thought her jealousy was funny. As they went about their travels, Dot would make tart observations about people, like, "She goes to church too much," and Crow would laugh and say, "Dot, you are an original." Dot was an entertainer and Crow was an enthusiastic audience. They were entirely unalike, and the best of friends. Dot felt closer to Crow in some ways than to her own sister.

———————

All the women in the apartment at Walter Reed Drive were getting and sending letters. Dot Braden corresponded often with both of her brothers, Teedy and Bubba. Curtis Paris's letters had dropped off, and she lost track of him. Dot wanted to dump George Rush but couldn't quite bring herself to do it. So she and George kept writing.

Over time, the letters from Jim Bruce began to be the most important. His letters were written on feather-thin airmail stationery, neatly folded in sixths, and addressed to "Miss Dorothy Braden." Like the other military men, he sent them through the Army Post Office system, which disguised GIs' overseas locations by using, as a return address, the APO address of the American processing station. The envelopes from Jim always had the distinctive airmail edging, striped like a barber's pole.

Sometimes Jim complained when he didn't hear from Dot for any length of time. Letters to soldiers overseas tended to get held up in transit, and the upshot was that letters sometimes arrived in jumbled bunches. During the long waiting period, Jim's letters would get somewhat pitiful and Dot would smile when she read them.

The two of them were figuring out their relationship, which, like so many during the war, was evolving purely through letters, with no phone calls, no in-person visits.

As early as the beginning of 1944, Jim had floated the idea of marriage, and Dot struggled to decide whether she wanted to settle down, and if so, when, and with whom. She went back and forth. But here was the good thing about Jim Bruce: He didn't nag Dot. He told her he respected her decision not to get engaged. But he didn't give up either.

From time to time Dot took the train home to Lynchburg, and sometimes she glimpsed WAVES making the same journey. Loads of girl sailors would pile on. Sitting in her seat, if she was lucky enough to get one—once, she had to make the trip standing on an outside platform, along with

Crow and Liz and Louise, getting covered with smoke—she thought enviously that the Navy women in their uniforms looked very smart. Unlike the WAVES, she and her Arlington Hall colleagues were largely unrecognized for their war service. They were not honored or celebrated, and nobody asked them to model in fashion shows. People in her family knew Dot was doing something for the war, but they assumed it was secretarial and low-level. She could not even tell her mother the truth.

Even as she admired the Navy women's outfits, it never occurred to Dot that the WAVES might be engaged in the same war work that she was, trying—just as she was—to break the codes that would bring the boys home.

The very thought that so many young women were all working the same top secret job never crossed her mind. Nor was she aware that the competition between the US Navy and the US Army had come to a head as the Army struggled to match the Navy's efforts in the Pacific Ocean.

The Navy women broke enemy naval codes used across the world's major oceans.

CHAPTER TWENTY-THREE

Department K

August 1944

Every time there was a new code break or a big military assault in the Pacific, the US Army Signal Corps went out and scooped up more women like Dot and Crow. They were all given aptitude tests and rated as "clerical," "technical," or "analytic" when they arrived. Analytic work was the most difficult. It was the category both Dot and Crow had been chosen for.

As the Japanese coped with their changing island situation, the ex-schoolteachers had to cope with Japanese cryptanalytic changes. During 1944, there were thirty thousand water-transport-code messages received each month. This meant breaking a thousand messages a day. In August 1944, the Japanese began using a new additive, new codebooks, a new square, and new indicator patterns. Staying abreast of these was Crow's department. Crow with her math skills had been assigned to the "research unit," which did the ongoing analysis that enabled Dot to do the active processing work. Dot didn't know that, nor did Crow.

The schoolteachers working 2468 got a bit of specialized training. In a ten-day course, code breakers learned to compare messages such as

4 Oct 1944: 8537 1129 0316 0680 1548 2933
4860 9258 4075 4062 0465

6 Feb 1945: 5960 1129 1718 6546 1548 3171
0889 9258 4075 4062 0465

6 Mar 1945: 7332 1129 1718 3115 1548 8897
7404 9258 4075 4062 0519

and to see that these messages were relayed about the same day every month. They also saw that certain code groups reappeared in the same place and probably represented a stereotype word, a word that appeared often.

The 2468 code breakers operated on a twenty-four-hour basis. There were three shifts—day, swing, and graveyard— and women rotated between them. One report noted that the Japanese Army unit "probably handles the most enemy traffic for deciphering of any agency in the world."

The women in Department K—Dot's unit—worked well. Department K produced all kinds of shipping intelligence, foretelling what Japanese units were about to receive oil or gasoline; what ships were in a given harbor; what convoys were getting ready to sail and where they were headed.

On May 3, 1944, Department K read a series of messages indicating the noon positions through May 8 of fifteen ships headed for New Guinea. Shortly thereafter, the US Navy sank four of them. In September 1943, the *New York Times* reported on a successful Pacific engagement in which "our strongly escorted medium bombers attacked an enemy convoy of five cargo ships and two destroyers." The *Times* reader probably thought it was "chance" that the bombing mission found the convoy. Not so. In fact, a message had been intercepted and read two weeks earlier.

November 1943, one month after Dot's arrival at Arlington Hall, marked the war's most devastating month for Japanese shipping. US subs sank forty-three ships and damaged twenty-two. In December, American subs sank thirty-two ships and damaged sixteen.

Behind the success of the US Navy were the code breakers. US submarines were kept so busy by information from decoded messages that they could not handle all the convoys they were alerted to. Over at the Naval Annex, the assembly line of WAVES identified the movements of marus supplying the Japanese Navy. Findings from both operations found their way to the submarine captains, who could hardly keep up with the bounty of intelligence.

The devastation of Japan's shipping had a huge impact. Soldiers were deprived of food and medicine. Aircraft did not get spare parts and could not launch missions. Troops did not reach the places they were sent to as reinforcements. When the Japanese Eighteenth Area Army attempted to convince Japanese Army headquarters that it was possible to send them much-needed supplies, their messages laid out the shipping routes and sealed their doom. Only 50 percent of ships reached the destination; only 30 percent got home.

By mid-1944, Japan was isolated from its overseas sources of raw materials and petroleum, leaving its armed forces unable to operate with any kind of strength or confidence. Its outlying bases were weakened by lack of reinforcements and supplies and fell victim to US air, land, and sea assaults.

Code-breaking intelligence also made it seem to the Japanese that there were more American submarines in the Pacific than there really were. "In early 1945 it was learned from a Japanese prisoner of war that it was [a] common saying in Singapore that you could walk from that port to Japan on American periscopes. This feeling among the

Japanese was undoubtedly created, not by the great number of submarines on patrol, but rather by the fact, thanks to communications intelligence, that submarines were always at the same place as Japanese ships."

Arlington Hall worked closely with "Central Bureau Brisbane," its satellite unit in Australia, and with Australian and New Zealander code-breaking allies. The breaking of all the Japanese Army codes contributed to the success of Operation Cartwheel, General MacArthur's island-hopping campaign. MacArthur knew about supplies, troop training, promotions, convoy sailings, reserves, reinforcements, and impending Japanese attacks.

By May 1944, messages translated by Arlington Hall had alerted the US Army to changes in the Japanese Army, helping identify new armies, divisions, and brigades. The staff knew how many planes the Japanese Army air forces had and the condition of the railroads; they knew about shipping losses and were able to keep a running tally.

As the Americans planned to retake the Philippines, code breakers fed them information on reinforcements, plans to check US air activity, units engaged in battle, Army supplies, and reinforcement problems.

The code breakers also responded to requests from American military intelligence. "When they were planning some major moves against the Japanese—either against some of the islands or the last big move that they were planning was, of course, the invasion of the Japanese mainland—they would come and ask us, if possible, to concentrate on messages from one or two certain places," remembered Solomon Kullback. As a result, MacArthur "wasn't going in blind into a lot of these areas he invaded." He had advance knowledge about how many Japanese soldiers his forces would meet on a particular island, how sick or healthy those soldiers were, and how well supplied they were with weapons and ammunition.

In this way, code breaking proved instrumental in keeping American men alive. George C. Kenney, MacArthur's air corps commander, was able to triumph in the air and shorten the ground war. Code breaking enabled the destruction of Japanese aircraft in Wewak, New Guinea, in August 1943, and in Hollandia, New Guinea, in March and April 1944, making MacArthur's "greatest leapfrog operation" possible along the northern New Guinea coast. In November 1944, Arlington Hall decoded messages saying that two Japanese convoys contained troops to reinforce the Philippines. The US Navy sank at least six of the ships and disabled one, and one caught fire.

Joe Richard, the young officer working in the Australian unit who spotted the digit pattern that led to the break in 2468, told later of how the recovery of a codebook on

Okinawa, in June 1945, "led to reading about the Japanese Army's preparations to fight against any landing on their home islands. These were so extensive, involving every Japanese, that the Allied general staff estimated (based on experience at Iwo Jima and Okinawa) that one million casualties might be expected by our Allied forces." Richard believed those preparations were what led President Truman to use the atom bomb rather than invade the country.

In the summer of 1944, the US military retook Guam. The Americans got an intercept station up and running again, and Dot Braden, sitting at her wooden worktable, began to get a lot of intercepts from Guam. Never having been anywhere near the Pacific Ocean, she always visualized Guam as a tiny little island with a single palm tree on which a lone American GI sat, sending intercepted messages over teletype, which ended up in her hands.

Even from Washington, DC, Dot could tell that things were going much better for the Allies in the Pacific, thanks in part to the efforts of women like her and Crow and Miriam. "Now we're getting somewhere," she would think as she ran between the table where she worked and the console where Miriam put together the overlaps. She and the other women knew that ship sinkings were the result of their work.

During the course of 1943 and 1944, while Dot Braden ran to and fro between her table and the overlappers' console, nearly the entire Japanese merchant fleet was wiped out. Beginning in 1943, not having enough food and medicine became the common lot of the Japanese soldier. Officials later estimated that two-thirds of Japanese military deaths were the result of starvation or lack of medical supplies.

The code breakers did not feel sadness or guilt. America was at war with Japan; Japan had started the war; the lives of American men were at stake, not to mention America itself. It was that simple.

So Dot did the best she could, giving her all on every shift, using the stereotypes to get started, doing mental math, going to the filing cabinets to retrieve duplicate messages, running over to Miriam and ignoring her disrespect.

"It was like a puzzle," she remembered later. "We were getting somewhere. I was proud I was doing it."

Dot would sometimes hear high-ranking military officers talking, saying that things were going well. She had never thought the United States might lose the war, even when the news was grim. Now she could feel that the progress of the war was on the upswing.

SIGABA

During World War I, the United States used manual code and cipher systems to keep their information secure. By World War II, most nations enciphered their secrets using machines. The United States was no different.

In the 1930s, the US Army's William Friedman and his assistant, Frank Rowlett, wanted to design a cipher machine that was easy to use and had key settings that were simple to change. And, of course, it had to be impossible to break.

They worked with the Navy to create a machine that both the Army and the Navy could use. The Army called it SIGABA; the Navy, ECM (Electric Cipher Machine) II. SIGABA used rotors, like the German Enigma machine, to encipher messages. SIGABA, however, had three banks of five rotors each. The second and third banks controlled the setting of the first.

SIGABA was the most secure cipher machine of World War II and was never broken. The military continued to use it into the 1950s. Today, this field is called cybersecurity.

CHAPTER TWENTY-FOUR

"Enemy Landing at the Mouth of the Seine"

June 1944

By the middle of 1944, as a result of his many victories, Adolf Hitler's Germany controlled the entire northwestern coast of Europe from Norway and Denmark to the South of France. That also meant Germany would have to somehow protect the coast from an Allied invasion—something the Allies knew they would have to do if they were going to win the war. The Nazis did not know when or where an invasion would happen, and so they built defenses all along the coast.

Code breaking helped the Allies discover where Germany's weaknesses were and where to plan the invasion. In

November 1943, the Purple machine at Arlington Hall rattled out one of the most valuable contributions that Hiroshi Oshima, the Japanese ambassador to Nazi Germany, made to the American intelligence effort. It was a complete description of German defenses along the coast of France, what the Germans called their Atlantic Wall.

Oshima made it clear: The Atlantic Wall had sections that were less well protected than others. It would make an invasion difficult, but not impossible.

"Naturally it cannot necessarily be expected that they [the Allies] could be stopped everywhere along the line," he wrote. "But even if some men did succeed in getting ashore, it would not be easy for them to smash the counterattack of the powerful German Reserves, who can rally with lightning speed."

Oshima provided the kind of intelligence the Allies needed to defeat the Nazis. He noted that "the Straits area is given first place in the German Army's fortification scheme and troop dispositions." By this he meant the Strait of Dover, which is the narrowest part of the English Channel—the point where the crossing is shortest—connecting Dover in England to Calais, the French port. "Normandy and the Brittany peninsula come next in importance," his message continued. He detailed where German troops were located, and their strengths and numbers.

All of this was deciphered by the Purple unit at Arlington Hall. If code breaker Genevieve Grotjan (who broke the Purple cipher) had tied it up with a ribbon, she could not have made a prettier present to Allied military commanders. The messages were supplemented by others sent through the Japanese naval attaché's machine being read by Frank Raven and his team at the Naval Annex. What they learned found its way to the military officers planning D-Day, the day the Allies would invade France. So did German Army Enigma messages read with the help of the Navy's bombe machines. At Bletchley Park in England, code breakers broke a long message from German field marshal Erwin Rommel, describing defenses along the Normandy beaches.

Together, the intelligence from these code-breaking efforts helped Allied commanders decide that they would concentrate their forces away from Calais and make their D-Day landing in Normandy.

For the D-Day attack to succeed, the Germans had to be taken by surprise. The Allies needed to be sure the Germans did not figure out what was happening in time to send reserve troops from other areas to help defend Normandy. One way to make that happen was by creating what

Winston Churchill called a "bodyguard of lies" to protect the truth about the exact time and place of the landings.

And so, in the months running up to the invasion, the Allies created a brilliant deception program—Operation Bodyguard—to confuse the Germans. They wanted the Germans to believe that Allied forces were bigger and more spread out than they actually were, and that an invasion of Europe would take place in several places at the same time.

They wanted the Germans to believe that the central attack would come in the region around Calais. So the Allies created a "phantom army," a fictitious force to throw the Germans off the scent. Double agents made false radio reports to Germany, spreading the word that the fake army was massing for an attack. But for a fake army to seem truly convincing, it needed something else: fake communications.

The Allied commanders had to assume that the Germans were monitoring radio traffic to figure out who was moving where. There was no way the American, British, and Canadian units could be sure that the Germans did not pick up their transmissions. Even if the Germans didn't break their code, the enemy could learn a lot by analyzing radio traffic. It could reveal where the Allied troops were and where they were headed.

The Allies' solution? Fill the airwaves with fake traffic.

The Allies created two phantom armies. One existed to make the Nazis believe that an Allied force in Scotland was getting ready to invade Norway. The goal of that trick was to persuade the Germans to keep the troops that were stationed in Norway where they were, and not send them to France once the real landing began.

The other phantom army was known as the First US Army Group, or FUSAG, and it was supposedly led by General George Patton. Patton's fictitious FUSAG was supposed to be massing in England, to make an attack on the Pas de Calais. Patton *was* in England, but the First Army did not exist.

It was key that the Germans not only believe in Patton's fake FUSAG but also continue to believe in it even after D-Day. The Germans had to think a Normandy invasion was intended to distract attention from the big one coming in the Pas de Calais. If they believed that, the Germans would keep most of their army in the Pas de Calais. That would give the Allies time to establish a base in Normandy and begin the liberation of France.

For a fake army to be believed, it had to send the same kind of radio traffic that a real army would send. The radio traffic had to begin well before the attack was launched, and it had to stay in place for weeks after. Creating this traffic was a very important job. Much of it would be done by the women at Arlington Hall.

American and British lives were at stake. The women knew that there could be no mistakes.

At Arlington Hall, the staff of eight thousand did more than break enemy messages. They also encoded American traffic and made sure it was secure. They worked hard to avoid the sorts of stereotypes and predictable repetitions that had allowed them to break Japanese and German codes.

A whole section of Arlington Hall, staffed mostly by the Women's Army Corps (WACs), was devoted to "protective security." The women operated the SIGABA machines, America's version of the Enigma. Unlike the German Enigma, the SIGABA was never cracked. The WACs at Arlington Hall studied American message traffic, looking for "cryptographic error."

In order to create fake traffic, the women had to understand every last thing about real traffic. They made charts and graphs to study American communications in specific regions, at specific times, during specific events. Then they began sending out dummy traffic in the months before the D-Day landing, as Patton's fictitious First Army began to gather in England. Meanwhile, double agents were hard at work telling Germany that FUSAG was getting ready to assault the Pas de Calais.

The plan worked. On June 1, 1944, Baron Oshima sent a message to Tokyo over the Purple circuit. The message revealed that Hitler expected Allied landings would take place in Norway and Denmark and on the French Mediterranean coast. Oshima added that Hitler expected the real Allied attack to come sailing through the Strait of Dover, toward the Pas de Calais.

It was exactly what the Allies had hoped.

———————————————

The Enigma team at the Naval Annex had known for several days that an invasion of France was about to begin. The bombes were pounding full force to break the German traffic. An air of suspense and tension hung heavy as the women waited, wondering when the landing would occur. It could happen anytime. Tonight, however, Ann White looked up at the gorgeous full moon as she walked to work.

Surely, she thought, the night would be too bright for a surprise landing across the English Channel.

But then, not quite two hours into her shift, her team received an intercepted message that suggested differently. The women ran the message through the M-9. Ann, knowing German, was able to read the words even before the Enigma message was taken upstairs and translated. It was sent by central German command to all U-boats on the circuit. "Enemy landing at the mouth of the Seine." All up and down the coast of France, the Enigma machines were spitting out the same message, warning their U-boats that the Allies had landed at the mouth of the Seine River in France. And in Washington, DC, the women read the words as quickly as the U-boat crews themselves.

D-Day was under way. After a weather-driven delay of more than a day, the night of June 6 had cleared enough to enable—barely—a nighttime crossing of the English Channel. The full moon gave the Allies the tide they wanted, and the storm that had been whipping up the channel subsided for just long enough to launch the ships. Nearly twenty-five thousand airborne troops dropped by parachute and glider into the fields above the beaches. The Normandy beach landings—the largest seaborne invasion in human history—were beginning. It was finally happening.

The Allies were invading France.

Courtesy of National Security Agency

Women ran the machines that attacked the German Enigma ciphers, maintained wall maps that kept track of U-boat locations and Allied convoys, and wrote intelligence reports that would be used by naval commanders.

CHAPTER TWENTY-FIVE

D-Day

June 1944

D-Day—the invasion of France—was finally under way. And now the traffic really started flowing into Ann White's Naval Annex unit. The next German message described thousands of Allied ships—nearly seven thousand warships, minesweepers, landing craft, and support vessels—filling the English Channel off the coast of Normandy. Nearly four thousand miles from where the women were working, full of hope and dread and curiosity—the ships brought more than 160,000 American, British, and Canadian soldiers and the weapons and supplies they needed to assault the shores of German-occupied France.

The women followed the D-Day message traffic all night, reading the invasion from the Germans' point of view. The Allied soldiers were braving the beach, scaling the cliffs. The women read into the morning and through the rest of that day. At 1:40 in the morning they were warned to "make no reference of any kind to the fact that we know about the invasion, even after the news comes out officially." All night the women bolted up and down the stairs, taking the messages to the translators one floor above. They felt excitement, relief, and horror. They knew how important the event was. But not how the Allies were doing. The messages told them some things, but there was so much more they wanted to know. How many men were dying? Were the Nazis counterattacking?

The women worked as hard as they could. In the twelve-hour period between seven thirty a.m. and seven thirty p.m. on June 6, the crews scored eleven jackpots on the bombe machines, as the Germans shared news about the invasion. The women learned that the French Resistance had acted swiftly to cut German communications. "Even seated at our desks," Ann White would later write, "we felt the power of our country."

The Normandy landings came as a complete surprise to the Germans—a surprise that saved an estimated 16,500 Allied lives. The Allies over the next weeks were able to establish a true base on the beaches of Normandy and then break out past the hedgerows and begin the liberation drive toward Paris.

At eight a.m. on the day of the invasion—afternoon

now, in France—a bleary Ann White finished her all-night shift and walked out of the Naval Annex. She and some of the other women code breakers slipped inside St. Alban's Church. D-Day was a great achievement. But somehow it did not seem cause for celebration, not yet. Going to church was the only way they could think of to honor the hundreds of thousands of men who had already been lost in the fight.

Ann would remember the Normandy invasion as one of the great moments of the war. She would also remember her wartime code-breaking service as the great moment of her life.

But for now, all she could do was pray for the souls of the dead.

———————

Up and down, up and down. Set the wheels on the spindles, program the machine, sit down, wait. Then up again. Set the wheels on the spindles. Program the machine. Sit down, wait. Days after the Normandy invasion, the WAVES worked the bombe machines as the messages kept pouring in.

Jimmie Lee Hutchison Powers worked her bombe bay all during the Normandy landing and its aftermath, and so did her hometown friend Bea Hughart. The two former

Oklahoma switchboard operators jumped up and down, changing wheels day after day, as the Allied soldiers began to fight their way toward Paris. All the while they knew that the men they loved were taking part in the action.

Jimmie Lee's husband, Bob Powers, had piloted one of the gliders supporting the Normandy landing. Gliders were towed by planes and released over fields and forests, carrying troops as well as weapons and even jeeps, which would be waiting for the paratroopers and the men coming up from the beaches. The gliders were known as "flying coffins" because of their flimsy structure and the danger of the work.

By now, every American knew that there was a particular look to a telegram that arrived announcing a military death. If the soldier was dead, blue stars surrounded the clear window box with the address. A few days after the invasion, Jimmie Lee got something that was not quite that. Her high school sweetheart and husband of one year, Bob Powers, had been downed over a French town near one of the glider landing areas. Her telegram said he was missing in action. There was a period of terrible uncertainty, and then in September, she got the worst news: Her husband was indeed dead. Bea Hughart's fiancé had been killed at D-Day as well. The two women had joined the Navy to try to save the lives of American men, especially the ones they knew and loved. Even while succeeding at the larger mission, they had failed at the personal one.

It was only now that Jimmie Lee understood the seriousness of the work she was doing. When she asked for leave to attend her husband's funeral in Oklahoma, her request was denied. There were other bombe operators getting the same telegrams, and they could not all be allowed to leave. Jimmie Lee stayed at her post. Her father died not long after. She was never able to go home to tell her own father good-bye.

There was so much loss even amid the victories. Ten months after D-Day, in April 1945, President Franklin Roosevelt died. The women sobbed, and the WAVES marched in a parade to honor him. People wondered whether the new president, Harry Truman, would be up to the job.

In many ways the remaining days of the war were the bloodiest and worst. In both war theaters, Axis leaders tried to make Allied victories as costly as possible in terms of lives lost. Japan hoped that if it could kill enough sailors, Marines, airmen, and soldiers launching attacks, the United States might negotiate for peace.

Their method was to kill themselves along with

thousands of Allied sailors. Japanese pilots flew their planes into US ships, exploding on impact. They were called kamikazes. There were attacks by suicide boats as well.

The code breakers did what they could to keep track of their loved ones. At the library unit in the Naval Annex, Georgia O'Connor was able to follow the USS *Marcus Island*, the escort carrier on which her brother was serving. She tracked the carrier through all of the war's final Pacific battles. The *Marcus Island* suffered kamikazes and near misses. Georgia's brother was in the radio room of the ship. She did not communicate with him personally, but she was able to tell her family he was safe, though she could not tell them how she knew this.

Others were not so lucky. Elizabeth Bigelow, recruited out of Vassar, had two brothers serving in the Pacific. One was in the Marines. Her other brother, Jack, was serving on the *Suwannee*, an escort carrier. Jack was the oldest son in the family, a golden boy whom everybody, Elizabeth most especially, adored. After Pearl Harbor, he enlisted in the naval reserve, and in 1942 he was inducted into the Navy, where he became a radar officer.

In late October 1944, the campaign to retake the Philippines began. The *Suwannee* participated in the Battle of Leyte Gulf, the battle to win back the Philippines. Leyte Gulf was the largest naval battle of the war. It was the first battle that saw organized attacks by kamikaze airmen. A kamikaze tore a hole in the flight deck of the *Suwannee*. The plane's bomb exploded and set off a terrible fire.

Elizabeth's family got the awful telegram. She was given leave to go home for two days. Her father's hair turned gray, it seemed to her, overnight. None of them ever recovered from the loss.

Some of the women broke messages warning about attacks before they happened but were helpless to prevent them. Fran Steen—a lieutenant now—was working her shift as watch officer when a message came in saying that the destroyer captained by her brother, Egil, was targeted for a kamikaze raid. Her team alerted the Navy, but there was no way to prevent the attack. Fran kept working, knowing that the only thing she could do was her job. The kamikaze struck and her brother's ship was sunk. At the time she thought Egil was dead. She later learned that he was one of only a few to survive, shielded in the spot where he had been standing.

Donna Doe Southall was one of two hundred WAVES officers staffing the code room where the Annex received US Navy dispatches with news about ship sinkings. She was looking through the Atlantic ship-sinking traffic when she saw one saying that her brother's ship had been sunk. She didn't know it at the time, but a third of the crew survived, and the British destroyer *Zanzibar* plucked her brother out of the ocean. He was taken to England, where he was treated for pneumonia and given donated clothing by the Red Cross.

For years, Donna's mother sent packages to the woman who donated those clothes. Fabric shortages in England lasted long after the war. One of the packages contained a blue dress Donna had worn as a bridesmaid, and a number of English girls got married in that same blue dress.

For her part, Donna married a naval officer after the war who was on a ship off the coast of Okinawa that was hit by a kamikaze. He was blown out of his shoes, thought to be dead, but regained consciousness and lived to have a family with her.

The Normandy Invasion

The Normandy invasion, also called Operation Overlord, began with D-Day (the code name for the first day of a military attack) on June 6, 1944. US, British, and Canadian forces landed on five separate beaches in Normandy, France.

The Allies knew that in order to defeat the Axis powers in Europe, they would have to invade France. But they had to decide when and where.

US code breakers—and the information they uncovered about Hitler's fortifications—were crucial to the decision to begin the assault on the beaches of Normandy, on the northwestern coast. The tricks the code breakers used to make Hitler believe that the main assault would come elsewhere saved thousands of lives. Even so, from D-Day through August 21 more than 225,000 Allied soldiers were killed or wounded. The Germans lost even more soldiers—240,000 were killed or wounded. Another 200,000 were taken captive.

By the end of August, northern France was liberated from the Germans, and the Allies began to push into Germany.

CHAPTER TWENTY-SIX

Teedy

December 1944

Teedy Braden was five years younger than Dot. The Braden siblings were close. They loved to tease each other. Teedy and Dot's other brother, Bubba, liked to check out Dot's boyfriends. The two brothers would hang around the front yard of 511 Federal Street, taking a close look at whoever was visiting their sister. The brothers also liked to climb onto crowded streetcars, at the other end from Dot, and loudly say things like, "Who would ever want to go out with that little girl with the permanent wave in her hair?" Dot likewise enjoyed teasing her brothers about their romantic lives.

Teedy Braden finished high school on a Friday in June 1943 and by Monday he was in the US Army. He started basic training at Camp Fannin in Texas. Within a year General Eisenhower needed men to reinforce the troops who landed at Normandy. So the Army sent Teedy to Camp Breckinridge, Kentucky, for more training. In July 1944, a month after D-Day, Teedy was still at Camp Breckinridge and was able to get a two-week furlough to go home to Lynchburg.

"I sure do hope that you won't [be] too busy to run down as I sho would like to see you," he wrote to Dot, but Dot was unable to get time off. He wrote her again after he got back to training camp. "How's everything, gal? . . . I sure would've like to have come up and stayed with you for a while but I reckon it would've upset my schedule a little."

On July 31 Teedy wrote Dot to say that he might be coming to Fort Meade, Maryland, in about two weeks. "If I do go it'll mean that it's the first step toward taking a boat ride which we've all been expecting soon." "Boat ride" meant sailing on a troop ship across the Atlantic and into the European fighting. "We'll all go as riflemen," he told her. His unit was practicing nighttime river crossings.

Teedy did make the trip to Fort Meade. He would soon be part of the 112th Infantry Regiment of the Twenty-Eighth Infantry Division. He was one of thousands of very young men shipped over to replace the men lost in the fighting during and after D-Day. These new men had been hastily trained and were not hardened to battle. Some veterans avoided them as green and inexperienced. They tended to "become casualties very fast," as one officer put it.

This was Teedy's situation. Dot's mother came up before he left, and she and Dot both went to see him off. With the Atlantic Ocean swept clear of U-boats, Teedy Braden made the ten-day Atlantic crossing to England, not yet twenty years old, sleeping in the bottom of the ship in a hammock slung from pipes.

Teedy entered some of the worst fighting American troops would experience in the European war theater. The Allies were pursuing the German Army, but the Nazi soldiers were putting up fierce resistance. Hitler was seeking one last, huge win.

At the beginning of November, Teedy's unit found itself caught in the Battle of Hürtgen Forest along the border between Belgium and Germany. Nazi troops laid mines and booby traps, strung barbed wire, and built bunkers amid the trees. Teedy's unit suffered extremely high casualties. At one point they were down to three hundred men from more than two thousand.

And it was just a warm-up. Barely two weeks later, the Germans attacked in what became known as the Battle of the Bulge. It was Hitler's last big roll of the dice, and the biggest, bloodiest battle the United States fought in Europe. And it was one of the war's worst intelligence failures. Allied code breakers had noticed a radio silence suggesting the Germans were planning an attack, but the military did not pay enough attention. The American soldiers were taken by surprise.

Teedy's division was one of those taken by surprise. It was short of both men and weapons. What was left of his unit sustained enormous casualties as the Germans tried to break through Allied lines. As Dot heard it later, her mother, Virginia, was visiting with friends in Lynchburg when she received the terrible message saying Teedy was missing in action.

Virginia Braden did not tell Dot. At Arlington Hall, the code breakers worked hard throughout the battle. At the Navy facility the bombes whirred away, and the women at Sugar Camp also knew the Battle of the Bulge was unfolding. Everyone worked overtime.

When the fog of war cleared, Teedy Braden had survived. Speaking years later, Teedy remembered jagged and shifting battle lines. At one point he and some other GIs found themselves behind enemy lines. "I was on an armored car, holding on to it for dear life," Teedy said. "As we come out the other side I see this German come out of the ditch carrying a Panzerfaust," which was a handheld rocket launcher. The German pumped it into the side of the armored car; Teedy was blown across the road and into a tree, where he was knocked out. When he came to, he saw burning tanks, burning ambulances, and green flares as German tanks fired into the sides of Allied vehicles. Nazi soldiers were running up and down shooting American men. Unarmed, Teedy nipped around a tree and spotted some fellow GIs moving cautiously through the forest. He joined them and they made their way through the woods, hitting the ground whenever the Germans opened fire.

"Then all of a sudden a .50-caliber machine gun in front of us opened up and we knew we had hit the [American] Eighty-Second Airborne," Teedy Braden remembered. Teedy started off in their direction, but he passed out again. An American tank crew scooped him out of the road and carried him to a château packed with weary men. He found a spot to sleep on the floor of a bathroom, wedged between a toilet and a wall. In the morning he got coffee and stood on the lawn, watching American bombers flying into Germany. It took a long time for survivors to get sorted and reequipped, having straggled in from many devastated units.

Teedy did not share any of this with the people back home. "I suppose that you've been kinda worried since I haven't had a chance to write you for some time," Teedy wrote Dot in January 1945. "I've only been able to write mom a couple of times." He explained that Christmas, for him, was a "kinda hectic one."

Being Teedy, he was still able to joke. He had taken French in high school because his big sister Dot had, and it was proving useful in Europe. He'd been able to eat a meal in a fine Belgian restaurant. "I can now snap my fingers and yell 'garcon' [waiter] with the best of them," he told her.

"Well, Dot, I just wanted to let you know that I am still percolating," he finished. He enclosed five Belgian francs as a souvenir and told her it was worth about twelve cents. "It sure is fancy money for .12, isn't it?" he said. "Well, I hope that all of you have a pretty fruity list of New Year's resolutions now. So long! Love, Teedy."

When he arrived safely home from Europe, Dot called their mother, and Virginia Braden got on a bus and raced up to Washington so that she could see for herself that Teedy was alive.

Teedy had survived the Battle of the Bulge, but thousands of others had not.

The Battle of the Bulge cost nearly twenty thousand American lives, but by the spring of 1945 the Allies had managed to regain their momentum. They crossed the Rhine River into Germany, which was being subjected to a heavy bombing campaign. On the eastern front, Russian soldiers overwhelmed the German invaders and pushed toward Berlin. As the Russians drew nearer, Adolf Hitler committed suicide in his bunker on April 30. It was now a matter of time. In Italy—one of the toughest, longest campaigns for the Western Allies—German soldiers were overthrown. Benito Mussolini, the Italian leader, was killed on April 28.

On May 7, 1945, Germany surrendered. The Allies had won the Battle of the Atlantic—and the European war.

The Enigma unit at the Naval Annex read a message from German admiral Dönitz to his surviving U-boat captains, which told them, "You have fought like lions... unbroken and unashamed you are laying down your arms after a heroic battle." As GIs liberated concentration camps, the world would learn the full horror that had unfolded.

Many of the code breakers and their families would never recover from the losses of sons and brothers and loved ones. But the boys in Europe—those who were left— were coming home. In Washington, conga lines pranced along the streets. Some of the WAVES went to the roofs of hotels to watch the celebrations. A number of code breakers would remember the magical experience of watching the nighttime lights, long dimmed for the war, come back on in the nation's capital. Dot, Crow, and Louise absorbed the happy news at the apartment on Walter Reed Drive, though their workload remained just as demanding.

While the war had ended in Europe, it still raged in the Pacific. The code breakers in the Naval Annex and Arlington Hall were still hard at work, and the need for secrecy was as great as ever.

The Atom Bomb

Soon after V-E (Victory in Europe) Day on May 8, 1945, the war against Japan began to reach its final stages. Japan, however, refused to surrender, and its people seemed to be ready to die rather than give up the fight.

The Allies knew that an invasion of Japan would be brutal and bloody. They estimated that as many as a million Allied soldiers would be killed or wounded in the assault. President Harry S. Truman decided to drop a new type of bomb—a bomb more powerful than anything that had come before—on two Japanese cities that were devoted to war work.

On August 6, 1945, an American B-29 bomber dropped the world's first atomic bomb over the city of Hiroshima. The explosion wiped out 90 percent of the city and immediately killed 80,000 people. On August 9, 1945, a second bomb was dropped over Nagasaki, leading to thousands more dead.

On August 15, the Japanese announced their surrender. The bombings had allowed the Allies to avoid an invasion and saved hundreds of thousands of Allied lives.

CHAPTER TWENTY-SEVEN

The Surrender Message

August 1945

The leaders of the United States, the United Kingdom, and the Soviet Union met at Yalta in the Soviet Union on February 11, 1945, to discuss the postwar peace in Europe. There and at later meetings in Potsdam, Germany, Allied leaders insisted on unconditional surrender. They wanted the Japanese to admit defeat and for the emperor to step down. The Japanese government refused.

On August 6, the *Enola Gay*, an American B-29 Superfortress plane, flew over the Japanese city of Hiroshima and dropped an atomic bomb. It was the first atomic bomb ever to be used in battle. On August 9, another atomic bomb was dropped, this one over Nagasaki. The Japanese said they would consider surrender but insisted that the emperor be allowed to remain.

Many women code breakers had brothers serving in Pacific units preparing to invade the Japanese homeland. Ruth "Crow" Weston's youngest brother was among them. Such an assault could cost as many as a million American lives. During the first half of August, kamikaze attacks continued against American warships and aircraft. At Arlington Hall, Japanese Army message traffic told of the number of Japanese soldiers waiting to fight against an invasion. The diplomatic traffic, however, was saying something slightly different.

───────────

The minute Ann Caracristi set foot in Arlington Hall on the afternoon of August 14, 1945, she knew something important was up. Excitement seemed to be rolling down the halls of the building. And there was no question where the tsunami of excitement was coming from: the language unit.

The Japanese-language translators were crucial to the work being done at Arlington Hall. There were never enough of them. The language unit read every diplomatic message that came into Arlington Hall, and so far there had been half a million.

For the past six months those communications had been intense and wretched. Japanese diplomats living in Europe reacted to what was happening in their homeland. The translators understood their fear and misery and even grew to feel attached to some of them.

The diplomatic ciphers coming into Arlington Hall included not only Purple messages, but those in other systems as well. Not every diplomatic missive was enciphered by the high-level Purple system. Other systems carried traffic about heavy industry, financial dealings, espionage, air raids, and commodities. One called JAH was used around the world and carried the largest volume of diplomatic traffic.

JAH was handled by a woman named Virginia Dare Aderholdt, who had spent four years in Japan. She knew JAH backward and forward. She could scan and decode and translate almost at the same time as messages came through the machine built to receive them.

The Arlington Hall translators had followed the conversations of Japanese officials. They knew what was taking place in captured territories whose Japanese-run governments were starting to weaken. Beginning in January 1945, the translators found themselves reading dispatches that reported on the raids over Tokyo by US aircraft.

The translators followed the movements of Ambassador

Oshima as he left Berlin and was captured in May. Message after message from Oshima and other Japanese diplomats in Europe said that Japan had best think about getting out of the struggle. Air raids on Japan were intense, and the diplomats in Europe were miserable when they thought of their homeland.

By midsummer, events began to move very fast. Japanese diplomats were having conversations about ending the conflict. In Bern, Switzerland, a Japanese banking official was having undercover conversations with Allen Dulles of the Office of Strategic Services (OSS), the US agency responsible for spy activity. Diplomatic messages helped the United States monitor side conversations the Soviets were having with the Japanese. When President Harry S. Truman was informed about one of these by Winston Churchill, he already knew about it, thanks to the quick work of Arlington Hall.

In early August, Arlington Hall translators started seeing traffic suggesting that the Japanese were planning to announce their intent to surrender. Because the two countries were at war, there was no direct communication between the United States and Japan. The surrender message would have to go through a few steps to reach the United States.

The message was sent from Tokyo to the Japanese ambassador in Switzerland, a neutral country. The ambassador then took the message to the Swiss foreign office. The Swiss passed it on to the United States.

The code breakers watched every step. They set up a special intercept net to snatch the message. They knew it was going to arrive in JAH.

On August 14, the whole translating unit was on pins and needles. People were afraid to go to lunch. Finally a message came through announcing the arrival of more messages. Soon, the one they were waiting for arrived.

The surrender message had to pass through two radio-transmitting stations to get to Switzerland. The Americans snatched it from the first and worked so fast that Virginia Aderholdt had it decoded and translated before the Japanese received it on the other end. Word got to the president as soon as they could get him a clean copy.

At Arlington Hall, the rule was that translators must keep the contents of all messages to themselves, and up to then, they had. But this time, staying quiet was not humanly possible. The Second World War was over.

The news spread throughout Arlington Hall, but it was too soon to let the world know. Everyone was gathered and asked to raise their right hands and take a vow of silence. Dot Braden was among them.

Japan had surrendered, but they couldn't reveal that news until the president announced it later that day. Dot felt excited and glad, but not surprised that the war was finally over. The truth surged inside Arlington Hall, bubbling to come out. But the code breakers kept it in.

At seven p.m., President Truman announced the Japanese surrender to a weary but overjoyed nation. Dot Braden, Ann Caracristi, Virginia Aderholdt, and the rest of the code breakers poured out of Arlington Hall. So did the women working at the Naval Annex. "The city exploded," recalled Elizabeth Bigelow. Lyn Ramsdell, one of the friends from the Navy's library unit, was sitting in a movie theater when a bulletin flashed across the screen. "Everybody just got up and left the movie, they were so excited, and the streets were just mobbed," she remembered. Outside, traffic was terrible: Cars were gridlocked, the buses were all full, people were shouting and dancing and singing. Trying to make her way back to the Naval Annex, Lyn ended up riding on the top of somebody's car. Other people perched atop trolleys, while above them, hotel residents flung toilet-tissue streamers out the windows. Groups ran arm in arm singing "Happy Days Are Here Again." A crowd tried to break into the White House grounds, shouting for the president: "Give us Harry!"

From Arlington Hall, thousands of people crossed the

river from Virginia into Washington. One of the Arlington code breakers, Jeuel Bannister, met one of the Japanese translators as they were all linking their arms and singing. She had never seen him before but sensed—correctly—that she had met her future husband. After that, she always referred to Victory over Japan Day (V-J Day) as "Victory for Jeuel" Day. The next day, August 15, Truman declared a two-day holiday to celebrate the surrender of Japan. They had done it. The Allies had won. The world war was over.

The Japanese messages dried up. There was nothing to do at Arlington Hall except crossword puzzles. On August 18, 1945, Brigadier General Preston Corderman gathered Arlington Hall employees into a grassy clearing. Ann Caracristi and her friends called his talk his "Here's your hat, what's your hurry" speech. The Arlington Hall code breakers were thanked for their service and told that it was their patriotic duty to get off the government payroll.

This seemed fair to Ann. She loved the work, but she could see that the government no longer needed her service. She returned home to Bronxville, where a family friend helped her get a job in the subscription office of the New York *Daily News*. It was her job to sift through data and pinpoint who the paper's subscribers were. It was not nearly as much fun as breaking codes. So Ann was delighted when she got a call from Arlington Hall. The code-breaking team wanted Ann back. She said yes immediately, and before she knew it she was headed back to Washington, where she would live for the rest of her life. It turned out that Arlington Hall was not being shut down.

In fact, it was just getting started.

Courtesy of Dorothy Braden Bruce

On a rare day off, Crow (far left), Dot (peeking out from behind the pole), and other Arlington Hall code breakers went to the beach.

CHAPTER TWENTY-EIGHT

Peace

December 1945

Jim Bruce returned from overseas in September 1945. After nearly two years of letter writing, Dot agreed to marry him. Dot "knew Jim was the one." Crow had started crying when she heard Jim Bruce was coming back. She was going to miss their easy friendship, their adventures, and their shared jokes.

The couple were married on December 29, 1945, in Lynchburg and took a short honeymoon in the North Carolina mountains. From there Jim had to travel back to Oklahoma. Leaving the Army took a while. Time seemed to be operating in slow motion.

Dot had not heard the "Here's your hat, what's your hurry" speech, or if she did, she ignored it. On December 14, Dot had taken a test evaluating her written French and did so well that she was put in the French decoding section, which was clearing up messages left over from the German occupation. She was making $2,320 a year, about $700 more than when she arrived, and far more than she had made as a teacher. Her evaluations all had been positive and she had won promotions.

While Jim was in Oklahoma, they both felt it made sense for Dot to keep her job. Housing was hard to come by, and the money would come in handy. But separation was hard on the newlyweds.

On January 31, 1946, Dot Braden Bruce resigned from Arlington Hall and prepared to travel to Oklahoma to join her husband. She sold her share of the furniture to Crow, who was keeping the one-bedroom apartment with her sister Louise. Louise was working as an astronomer at the Naval Observatory, and Crow was still working at Arlington Hall.

Union Station—so much more familiar than when she first arrived—was chaos. The ticket office told Dot she could get a ticket as far as Cincinnati and then would have to take her chances. Crow came to see her off, and so did Dot's mother. Dot's memory of Crow as she left was of her best friend crying and calling out, "If you think I'm going to stay here all my life with Sister, you've got another think coming!"

Soldiers had not seen women in months. They all

wanted to talk to Dot as she traveled across the country. She never paid for a meal. One GI asked if she would get off the train and have dinner with his family. She told him she was married and he said they wouldn't care; his folks would just be happy to meet her. Another sat down next to her, pretended to fall asleep, and snuck his arm around her. A sailor made him move away. When she got to Cincinnati, helpful soldiers lifted her up and put her on the train to Oklahoma. Jim managed to get discharged over the course of a few weeks, and they moved to Richmond, where his prewar job was waiting for him.

In February 1946, Dot received a letter from what was now called the Army Security Agency, the new name for Arlington Hall. It thanked her for her wartime service. It also said, "You were entrusted with information which should not, under any circumstance, be revealed to unauthorized persons." This information "should not now, or at any future time, be revealed," it added. Dot would continue to keep her war work a secret, even from her new husband.

It was a nightmare finding housing after the war. Everybody in America needed a place to live. In Richmond, the newlyweds set up in an apartment with thin walls and a couple next door who argued and threw dishes. The government trucked in houses for veterans. Jim stood in line and they got one. The new neighborhood was a nice place to live. The women drank coffee and talked about their new babies. Nobody asked Dot what she had done during the war.

Dot's first child, Jimmy, was born prematurely. Jimmy cried almost nonstop. Crow came down from Washington and brought her flowers and got her through that awful time. Jimmy would grow up just fine and Dot and Jim had two more children, both daughters, everybody healthy and happy.

Crow stayed at Arlington Hall, but she couldn't tell Dot what top secret project she was working on. Several years later, Crow met a man, Bill Cable, who worked for the Veterans Administration. Crow would not marry him until Dot and Jim met him and gave him their stamp of approval.

Crow had continued working as a mathematician with other elite wartime code breakers at Arlington Hall. But when she and her husband started their family, Ruth resigned, even though she very much liked what she did.

Women were expected to quit work when they started having babies. The postwar US government made this clear, making films telling women it was important to leave their jobs and tend their households. The films pointed out that it was unnatural for women to be breadwinners, taking jobs from men. Quitting one's job became a matter of patriotism. And so, many of the wartime women workers did leave their jobs when they had children. Among them was Crow.

When Ruth "Crow" Weston Cable's daughters were growing up, they were under the impression that they were somehow related to Dot's son, Jimmy. The two former code breakers remained so close that their children assumed they were family.

Both women grew bored at home and went back to work when their children were in school. Dot became a real estate agent. Crow, still living in Arlington, took a job as a mapmaker. Crow loved maps, and she loved her work. She also worked the polls every Election Day. That day of commitment to democracy remained sacred to her.

———

A number of women code breakers who distinguished themselves during World War II went on to high posts at the new National Security Agency (NSA), which merged the Army and Navy code-breaking operations. But by far the majority of women at Arlington Hall and the WAVES Annex packed up and went home after the war.

Motherhood was the dividing line between brilliant women who stayed in the workforce and those who did not. The nation lost the talent that the war had developed. In the 1970s and 1980s, when women started entering the workforce in greater numbers again, women at the NSA would have to fight a battle for equality all over again.

For the women who left the field but wanted to continue working or studying, postwar opportunities were mixed. Women who served in the US Navy qualified for the GI Bill, which provided money for college to veterans, at least in theory.

The Navy women, however, often came up against the old idea that women are not suited for the highest levels of learning. Elizabeth Bigelow had been recruited by the Navy from Vassar. When she got out of the Navy she applied to three leading architecture schools. "In every case the response was the same," she recalled later. "We're sorry, but we are saving all our spaces for the men who have been in the armed services." So she married and raised a family with her husband. Elizabeth ended up running the computer system at the University of Cincinnati. She taught herself how to do it.

Dorothy Ramale, who grew up in Cochran's Mills, Pennsylvania, became an expert "reader" of enemy messages at Arlington Hall. She got a master's degree using the GI Bill, which meant she earned a higher salary working as a math teacher. She longed to visit every continent on earth, and she did, including Antarctica—twice.

Jimmie Lee Hutchison Powers, who lost her husband on D-Day, used the GI Bill to get a community college degree in cosmetology. She opened a salon back home in Oklahoma and supported herself and her widowed mother. After three years, she remarried.

Betty Bemis, the champion swimmer who worked at Sugar Camp, corresponded during the entire war with Ed Robarts, a bomber pilot whom she had not actually met. One day she was summoned to the phone. "Hi, Betty," he said. "I'm home." He asked her to fly to have Easter dinner with him and his aunt and uncle in Miami. Betty hitched a ride on a military plane to see him. Three days later, she agreed to marry him.

For some of the women, especially those who worked in top spots on the Enigma project, life after the war was harder. Louise Pearsall, who worked on Enigma, was tempted to stay on with the work after the war. But she was exhausted—mentally, emotionally, physically—and there was a boyfriend who had come back to Elgin, Illinois. She got discharged, returned to Elgin, and they broke up. She went to work but quit when she suffered a nervous breakdown. She married a wealthy man, but the marriage wasn't a happy one. She eventually would divorce her husband and take a job with IBM that she quite liked.

Betty Allen, one of the group of friends in the library unit at the Naval Annex, also had a hard time after the war. Most jobs went to men. Meanwhile her friends, mostly married, had new babies and were living isolated lives in small spaces. So the former cryptanalytic librarians came up with a solution to their loneliness. They would write a round-robin letter.

Here is how the round-robin letter worked: One former code breaker would write a letter about what was going on in her life. She would send it to a second woman, who would write her own letter. That second woman would send both letters to a third woman, who would write her own and send all three to a fourth. The thickening collection would travel full circle until it came back to the first woman, who would remove her old letter, write a new one, insert it, and send the collection around the circle again.

As of 2015, when I visited her, Ruth Schoen Mirsky was still writing to Lyn Ramsdell Stewart. They and one widowed husband were the only three left. When Lyn died, Ruth and the widower kept in touch.

Ruth still has the ribbon commemorating the special unit citation that all the women at the Naval Annex received after the war. When I asked to see it, she reluctantly agreed.

The women were instructed not to show it to anybody, and she still can't bring herself to let it be photographed.

The Navy women treasured that unit citation, but most never displayed it.

Fran Steen, the Goucher biology major who put aside her ambition to be a doctor, married a naval officer. She kept her pilot's license until she got pregnant. Her husband was killed in 1960, struck by lightning while playing golf. She got remarried to a naval submariner. She worked as a census taker, an artist, and a fashion model. She was always reluctant to talk about her wartime service. Eventually she did tell her son, Jed, about being a watch officer when they got the message that her brother's ship was hit by a kamikaze, and about learning to shoot and bringing the bombes back from Dayton.

Rear Admiral (ret.) David Shimp met Fran Steen Suddeth Josephson at a Charleston cocktail party. He had always heard her mentioned as one of the code breakers who cracked the messages that led to the shootdown of Yamamoto. He arranged for her to be given a surprise award at a dinner for cryptologic veterans. Her son, Jed, got her there without telling her what the meeting was for. As Fran was listening to the speech, she began to realize they were talking about her. Whenever Shimp tried to get her to share more details, though, she refused. When she did talk, she would dwell on the lives she hadn't been able to save, rather than the ones she had.

Over time public views changed about the war. One was not always well advised to mention what one had done. Jeuel Bannister Esmacher, the band director who worked at Arlington Hall, knew that a message she broke helped sink a convoy. She saw certain code words, hurried the message to the "big boys," and later heard over the radio that the ships had been sunk. At the time she felt proud. But when she started a family with the translator she met during the V-J Day celebration, Harry Esmacher, she thought about all the Japanese families who lost sons, and her feelings changed. She felt more sorrow. "There were Japanese that went down with that ship that had mothers and sisters and wives," she reflected when I spoke with her. "You think about that also, at this point. I did not think of that back then."

Jane Case Tuttle, the wealthy physicist's daughter, also got married after the war, and it was a disaster. She managed to end the marriage and found that the memory of working during the war gave her self-confidence. Late in life she married a man who had been madly in love with her during the war. When I visited her, she was living at an assisted-living facility in Maine, an ardent supporter of the presidential candidacy of Bernie Sanders. Because she could no longer walk easily, she would sit in a recliner and throw clean, balled-up socks at the television when a politician she hated came on.

Anne Barus Seeley also married; she never pursued a career in international relations, but she did work in other capacities, including running a weaving business and teaching. In her mid-nineties, she was still sailing and kayaking near her home on Cape Cod.

Many of the code-breaking women helped advance the feminist movement—through their postwar employment, but also, sometimes, their postwar dissatisfaction.

Courtesy of Dorothy Braden Bruce

Dot and Crow's friendship remained so strong that
Crow insisted that Dot and her husband, Jim Bruce,
come to Washington to meet her own fiancé, Bill Cable,
and give their stamp of approval before she would
marry him. From left to right: Bill, Crow, Dot, and Jim.

The Mitten

On a bright day in January 2016 a line of sedans, SUVs, and pickup trucks files into a cemetery in the northern Virginia foothills. The bundled-up mourners are wearing hats and gloves, picking their way across the soft ground to sit in folding chairs set up in rows under an awning. The group consists of family, neighbors, well-wishers, and members of the US intelligence and national security community. They have come to pay their respects to the woman who rose to become the first female deputy director of the National Security Agency (NSA)—Ann Caracristi.

Ann, who died at ninety-four, kept her razor-sharp intellect till the end. And she kept her sense of humor. She had worked on some of the toughest code-breaking challenges in the post–World War II years. Her first assignment was working ciphers about Soviet weapon systems. She would move on to breaking East German ciphers. It was difficult and serious work at a difficult and serious time.

Ann had come a long way from the bobby-soxer who washed her hair with laundry soap. During her career she was seen as fair and smart and tough. She worked with top military men and was respected by all of them. She received many honors during her career, including the National Security Medal and the Distinguished Civilian Service Award, the Department of Defense's highest civilian honor.

Dot Braden Bruce, of course, was one of those women who left the workforce when she married and had children (at least until her children were settled in school). In 2018, she lives in an assisted-living facility on the outskirts of Richmond, Virginia. At ninety-eight, she keeps her French skills sharp by chatting with caregivers from French-speaking West Africa.

Her life has come full circle, and once again she is living in a one-bedroom apartment. Crow died in 2012, Jim Bruce in 2007. Dot herself is still lively.

Looking back, Dot wonders sometimes why she decided to marry Jim Bruce rather than George Rush. "My life could have turned out very differently," she reflects. Make no mistake; she felt she made the right choice. George Rush was a perfectly nice man. But she didn't want to move to California. She is so glad she took the train to Washington and embarked on her code-breaking service together with her friend Crow Weston Cable. "I wouldn't take anything for it," she says. She thinks what tipped the balance in favor of Jim Bruce was the fact that he was steady and kind. And persistent. And he had a good sense of humor.

And, she reflects, "he wrote me all those darling letters."

After the war, Dot told nobody what she did, maintaining her vow of secrecy. At some point, maybe fifty years after the war ended, she started giving hints. Her family did not believe her—her brother Bubba said it was "just a little job and I was trying to make it a big deal," she remembers now. But then they started to believe her, or sort of. Her grandchildren liked to say that Dot single-handedly broke the Japanese codes.

Memories come at odd times. Dot was reading aloud to one of her great-grandchildren a children's book called *The Mitten*, in which forest animals take refuge from a snowstorm by climbing, one by one, into a cast-off woolen mitten. So many animals climb in that one sneeze is enough to eject all of them. Reading it, she could not help but think of the Arlington apartment and all the girls who stayed in that one-bedroom place.

Her son, Jim, has always been intrigued by her wartime code-breaking service. As kids, he and his sisters used to go up in the attic and read the letters their dad wrote to their mother. His sentimental side was a revelation. But they never could get their mother to tell them details about what she did. Now she has gotten the okay from none other than the NSA and has been assured that it's fine to tell her story: The long-ago ban was lifted several decades ago. The government would *like* her to tell her story. But she still has her doubts. She cannot quite believe it after all these years.

On a Wednesday afternoon in 2014, during the first interview for this book, Jim, her son, is sitting in an upholstered wing chair in her one-bedroom apartment. "Let it rip, Mom!" he urges. By now so many male code breakers have written their memoirs: Edwin Layton and Frank Rowlett and others, with book titles like *And I Was There* and *The Story of Magic*. Dot relaxes, a bit, about telling the part she played in this dramatic story, and Jim listens as his mother begins to talk. She mentions Miriam the overlapper—awful Miriam!—and claps her hand to her mouth. Never has she uttered the word "overlap" outside the confines of Arlington Hall.

Even now, it has the feeling to her of something illicit, something forbidden, something dangerous and important, no matter how long ago this all occurred. It feels as if an enemy might still be at the window, listening in.

ACKNOWLEDGMENTS

My grateful thanks go, first, to the women who did this work during the war. Most took the secret to their graves, and it is too late, unfortunately, to thank them in person. I also am grateful to the women who consented to be interviewed for this book, many in circumstances that were not easy. Janice Martin Benario broke her wrist the night before our interview, so we conducted it in a hospital emergency room in Atlanta. Dot Braden Bruce took me to lunch, met with my own family, and always walked me to the door despite using a walker. Anne Barus Seeley invited my daughter and me to her Cape Cod home and drew columns on a piece of paper showing how she recovered additives. Ruth Schoen Mirsky brought out her scrapbooks. Viola Moore Blount shared recollections by email. Dorothy Ramale and Edith Reynolds White were confined to wheelchairs during our meetings, and always dressed smartly. Suzanne Harpole Embree shared memories over lunch at the downtown DC Cosmos Club. When the Metro broke down, she walked several blocks and stood in line for the bus. Jo Fannon shared pamphlets she had saved for more than seventy years. Jane Case Tuttle wore the most awesome leopard-print bathrobe and gave me a gift bag of clean balled socks to throw at the television whenever a politician said something inane. It was easy to understand how women with this much spirit and fortitude helped the Allies win the war.

I also would like to thank the women in my family—my mother and grandmothers—who attended college. I still recall coming upon my grandmother Anna's old zoology notebooks from Hood College; that kind of example of academic achievement makes an impression on a young girl. In addition, I would like to thank the many historians and archivists who helped me navigate their fine collections, and family members who facilitated interviews and provided recollections. I am grateful to my book agent, Todd Shuster of Aevitas Creative, who provided every kind of support and guided me into the office of Paul Whitlatch and Mauro DiPreta at Hachette Books. At Little, Brown Books for Young Readers, executive editor Lisa Yoskowitz and editorial director Farrin Jacobs did a marvelous job of shepherding this edition into print and circulation, and Laurie Calkhoven wonderfully adapted the adult version. I'd also like to thank Anna Prendella, Hannah Milton, Jen Graham, Eileen Ghetti, Karina Granda, Victoria Stapleton, Michelle Campbell, Stefanie Hoffman, Valerie

Wong, and Kristina Pisciotta, and as well as publisher and executive vice president Megan Tingley and associate publisher and vice president Jackie Engel. It has been such a pleasure to work with everyone on this fine and committed team.

TIMELINE

World War II lasted for almost six years and involved nearly every country on five continents. The timeline that follows outlines some of the key events.

1939

SEPTEMBER 1   Nazi Germany invades Poland in a massive attack. Within weeks, Poland surrenders.

SEPTEMBER 3   France and Great Britain declare war on Germany following the attack on Poland.

SEPTEMBER 5   The United States declares that it will remain neutral.

1940

APRIL 9   Nazi troops invade Denmark and Norway.

MAY 10   The Nazi invasion of Belgium, the Netherlands, Luxembourg, and France begins. Within a few weeks, all but France surrender.

MAY 26   The evacuation of Dunkirk begins. British and French forces appear to be cut off, but over the next nine days more than three hundred thousand soldiers manage to avoid capture by the Nazis in a famous evacuation using fishing boats, yachts, lifeboats, and anything else that could float.

JUNE 22   France officially surrenders to Germany.

JULY 10   Germany begins nightly bombings over Great Britain in what will come to be called the Battle of Britain.

SEPTEMBER 20   Genevieve Grotjan finds the key to cracking the Japanese Purple machine, giving the United States access to all of Japan's diplomatic communications.

SEPTEMBER 27   Germany, Italy, and Japan sign a pact to support one another and become the Axis powers.

1941

JUNE 22   Germany invades its former ally, the Soviet Union. Within a few weeks, the Soviet Union joins Great Britain and becomes one of the Allied nations.

DECEMBER 7   The Japanese bomb Pearl Harbor in Hawaii.

DECEMBER 8   The United States, Great Britain, and Canada declare war on Japan.

DECEMBER 11   Germany and Italy declare war on the United States.

1942

FEBRUARY 15   Japan captures Singapore.

MAY 12   After several months of hard combat, Japan captures the Philippines.

MAY 14   President Franklin Roosevelt signs the Women's Army Auxiliary Corps (WAAC) bill into law.

MAY 26   Japan defeats the British in Burma and takes over that country.

JUNE   College graduates begin arriving in Washington, DC, to take up their code-breaking responsibilities.

JUNE 7   The Allies defeat Japan in the Battle of Midway, thanks in large part to Allied code-breaking efforts. The battle marked a turning point in the war.

JULY 21   Congress establishes the women's naval reserve— the WAVES. President Roosevelt then signs Congress's bill into law.

1943

FEBRUARY 2   German troops surrender in the Soviet Union. It is the first major defeat of Hitler's army.

FEBRUARY 7   After months of hard fighting, the last of the Japanese soldiers evacuate Guadalcanal in the western Pacific.

APRIL 18   Thanks to the work of US code breakers, the Allies are able to carry out Operation Vengeance over Bougainville Island in Papua New Guinea. Japan's admiral Isoroku Yamamoto, the mastermind behind the attacks on Pearl Harbor, is shot down and killed.

MAY 13   The United States and Great Britain achieve a major victory over Germany in North Africa.

SEPTEMBER 8   Italy surrenders to the Allies.

1944

JUNE 6   D-Day. After months of planning and false radio traffic to mislead the Germans, the invasion of France begins.

OCTOBER 26   Japan's Navy is defeated by the Allies in the Battle of Leyte Gulf, near the Philippines. It is the first battle that includes organized attacks by kamikaze airmen and is the largest naval battle of the war.

DECEMBER 16   In a last desperate attempt to avoid defeat, Hitler's forces attack Allied troops in the Ardennes forest in Belgium. The Battle of the Bulge, the largest land battle of World War II, begins.

1945

JANUARY 25   The Battle of the Bulge ends with an Allied victory.

MARCH 26   After a monthlong battle, Allied troops capture the Pacific island of Iwo Jima.

APRIL 30   Adolf Hitler commits suicide.

MAY 7   Germany surrenders to the Allies, ending the war in Europe. The next day becomes an official holiday— V-E Day, or Victory in Europe Day.

AUGUST 6   The United States drops an atomic bomb on the Japanese city of Hiroshima. Immediately, between 60,000 and 80,000 people die. The death toll will rise to 135,000 in the coming months.

AUGUST 9   A second atomic bomb is dropped, on the city of Nagasaki. The death count reaches as high as 80,000 by the end of the year.

AUGUST 14   Japan surrenders. Code breakers in Washington, DC, anxiously await the formal messages.

SEPTEMBER 2   Japan formally surrenders to the Allies in Tokyo Bay aboard the USS *Missouri*.

CODE GIRLS GLOSSARY

additive: A number added to a code group to make the message harder to crack

alumnae: Women who have graduated from a particular college or university

ambassador: A diplomat working on behalf of his or her government in a foreign country

auditory dyslexia: A disorder that makes it difficult to recognize and understand certain sounds

barracks: A simple group of buildings put up quickly to house members of the military

boardinghouse: A house where one can rent rooms and meals are provided

bombe machines: Machines built to crack the German Enigma cipher by detecting a day's key settings

bridge: A card game

burn bags: Bags in which discarded papers were put to be burned

calisthenics: Exercises

capsize: To overturn, like a ship in the water

cipher: A secret message system in which a single letter or number is replaced by another single letter or number

civilian: A person who is not a member of the military

clandestine: Secret

code: A secret message system in which an entire word or phrase is replaced by another word, a series of letters, or a string of numbers known as a "code group"

commission: To give military rank and authority

communist: Someone who believes in the communist form of government, a government in which property and goods are owned by the people, and civil rights are controlled by one political party

compound: A fenced or walled-in area with a group of buildings

counterpart: A person who has the same job as another in a different office or organization

crib: An educated guess about what a coded message says, used to help break the code or cipher

cryptanalysis: The art and science of breaking codes and ciphers

cryptography: The art and science of making codes and ciphers

cryptology: Both making and breaking codes and ciphers

decipher: To make out the meaning of a secret message written in cipher

decode: To make out the meaning of a coded message

destroyer: A small, fast warship

diplomat: Someone who conducts negotiations between nations

dispatch: An important message, usually sent by a diplomat or a member of the military

encipher: To change a message into a cipher

encode: To change a message into a code

fascist: Someone who believes in the fascist form of government, in which a dictator controls the government and disagreement is not allowed

fleet: A group of warships under a single command

flotilla: A fleet of ships

fortifications: Temporary structures built to defend a place or position

hypothesis: An educated guess based on evidence

indicator: A code group that specifies which part of an additive book has been used to further encipher a message

intelligence: Information collected for military and political purposes

intercept: A message that has been captured, or intercepted, from an enemy's communications

invasion: The act of invading, or entering, a country using military force

mess: A meal

Morse code: A code made up of dots and dashes, or long and short sounds, that represent letters and numbers

muster: To gather as a group

orientation: Training and information for a new job

pacifist: Someone who is against conflict, especially war

radar: A device that detects the positions of things, like ships and airplanes, using radio signals

recruit: A member of the armed forces; new soldiers signed up at recruiting stations

satellite unit: A small group working apart from the main organization

segregation: Separating a race or group from the rest of society

sexism: Discrimination based on gender

sonar: A method for locating objects underwater, like submarines, using sound waves

translator: Someone who can change a message from one language into another

transmission: A coded message sent by radio

transmit: To send a message, often using radio signals

WAAC: Women's Army Auxiliary Corps

WAC: Women's Army Corps

WAVES: Women Accepted for Volunteer Emergency Service (for the Navy)

BIBLIOGRAPHY

Selected Interviews

John "Teedy" Braden, in Good Hope, Georgia, December 1, 2015

Dorothy "Dot" Braden Bruce, in Midlothian, Virginia, between June 2014 and April 2017

Ann Caracristi, at her home in Washington, DC, numerous between November 2014 and November 2015

Dorothy Ramale in Springfield, Virginia, May 29 and July 12, 2015

Anne Barus Seeley in Yarmouth, Massachusetts, June 12, 2015

Nancy Dobson Titcomb in Springvale, Maine, October 1, 2015

Jane Case Tuttle, in Scarborough, Maine, September 30, 2015

Clyde Weston, by telephone, October 9, 2015

Kitty Weston, in Oakton, Virginia, April 10, 2015

Edith Reynolds White, in Williamsburg, Virginia, February 8, 2016

Manuscript and Archival Sources

National Archives and Records Administration II in College Park, Maryland

National Archives and Records Administration Personnel Records Center in St. Louis, Missouri

Library of Congress Veterans History Project in Washington, DC

Betty H. Carter Women Veterans Historical Project, Martha Blakeney Hodges Special Collections and University Archives, The University of North Carolina at Greensboro, North Carolina

William F. Friedman Papers and Elizebeth Smith Friedman Collection at George C. Marshall Foundation Library in Lexington, Virginia

National Cryptologic Museum Library in Fort Meade, Maryland

Naval History and Heritage Command Ready Reference Room in Washington, DC

Personal Archives of Deborah Anderson in Dayton, Ohio

Dayton History in Dayton, Ohio

Winthrop University Louise Pettus Archives

Center for Local History, Arlington Public Library, Arlington, Virginia

Historical Society of Washington, DC

Wellesley College Archives in Wellesley, Massachusetts

Schlesinger Library at Radcliffe Institute for Advanced Study in Cambridge, Massachusetts

Smith College Archives in Northampton, Massachusetts

Randolph College Archives in Lynchburg, Virginia

Jones Memorial Library in Lynchburg, Virginia

Pittsylvania County History Research Center and Library in Chatham, Virginia

Women Veterans Oral History Project, University of North Texas

Oral History Sources

Many people in this book—including many who are no longer alive—recorded their story, telling their recollections to an interviewer. I was able to read these oral histories online or in print, or listen to them discuss their wartime experiences in their own words, through the following collections:

National Security Agency Oral History Collection

Betty H. Carter Women Veterans Historical Project, Martha Blakeney Hodges Special Collections and University Archives, The University of North Carolina at Greensboro, NC

University of North Texas Oral History Collection

Library of Congress Veterans History Project

Books

Budiansky, Stephen. *Battle of Wits: The Complete Story of Codebreaking in World War II*. New York: Free Press, 2000.

Butler, Elizabeth Allen. *Navy Waves*. Charlottesville, VA: Wayside Press, 1988.

Carlson, Elliot. *Joe Rochefort's War: The Odyssey of the Codebreaker Who Outwitted Yamamoto at Midway*. Annapolis: Naval Institute Press, 2011.

Center for Cryptologic History. *The Friedman Legacy: A Tribute to William and Elizebeth Friedman*. National Security Agency, 2006.

Dalton, Curt. *Keeping the Secret: The Waves & NCR Dayton, Ohio 1943–1946*. Dayton: Curt Dalton, 1997.

DeBrosse, Jim, and Colin Burke. *The Secret in Building 26: The Untold Story of America's Ultra War Against the U-Boat Enigma Codes*. New York: Random House, 2004.

Ebbert, Jean, and Marie-Beth Hall. *Crossed Currents: Navy Women in a Century of Change*. Washington, DC: Brassey's, 1999.

Friedman, William. *Elementary Military Cryptography*. Laguna Hills, CA: Aegean Park, 1976.

———. *Elements of Cryptanalysis*. Laguna Hills, CA: Aegean Park, 1976.

———. *Six Lectures Concerning Cryptography and Cryptanalysis*. Laguna Hills, CA: Aegean Park, 1996.

Gildersleeve, Virginia Crocheron. *Many a Good Crusade*. New York: Macmillan, 1954.

Godson, Susan H. *Serving Proudly: A History of Women in the U.S. Navy*. Annapolis: Naval Institute Press, 2002.

Hart, Scott. *Washington at War: 1941–1945*. Englewood Cliffs, NJ: Prentice Hall, 1970.

Isaacson, Walter. *The Innovators: How a Group of Hackers, Geniuses, and Geeks Created the Digital Revolution*. New York: Simon & Schuster, 2014.

Johnson, Kevin Wade. *The Neglected Giant: Agnes Meyer Driscoll*. Washington, DC: National Security Agency Center for Cryptologic History, 2015.

Kahn, David. *The Codebreakers*. New York: Scribner, 1967.

———. *Seizing the Enigma: The Race to Break the German U-Boat Codes, 1939–1943*. New York: Houghton Mifflin, 1991.

Keegan, John. *The Second World War*. New York: Viking Penguin, 1990.

Kenschaft, Patricia Clark. *Change Is Possible: Stories of Women and Minorities in Mathematics*. Providence, RI: American Mathematical Society, 2005.

Kessler-Harris, Alice. *Out to Work: A History of Wage-Earning Women in the United States*. Oxford: Oxford University Press, 1982.

Kovach, Karen. *Breaking Codes, Breaking Barriers: The WACs of the Signal Security Agency, World War II*. Fort Belvoir, VA: History Office, U.S. Army Intelligence and Security Command, 2001.

Layton, Edwin T., Roger Pineau, and John Costello. *And I Was There: Pearl Harbor and Midway—Breaking the Secrets*. New York: Morrow, 1985.

Marston, Daniel, ed. *The Pacific War: From Pearl Harbor to Hiroshima*. Oxford: Osprey, 2005.

Mikhalevsky, Nina. *Dear Daughters: A History of Mount Vernon Seminary and College.* Washington, DC: Mount Vernon Seminary and College Alumnae Association, 2001.

Musser, Frederic O. *The History of Goucher College, 1930–1985.* Baltimore: Johns Hopkins University Press, 1990.

Overy, Richard. *Why the Allies Won.* New York: Norton, 1996.

Pimlott, John. *The Historical Atlas of World War II.* New York: Henry Holt, 1995.

Rowlett, Frank B. *The Story of Magic: Memoirs of an American Cryptologic Pioneer.* Laguna Hills, CA: Aegean Park, 1998.

Scott, Frances Lynd. *Saga of Myself.* San Francisco: Ithuriel's Spear, 2007.

Smith, Michael. *The Debs of Bletchley Park and Other Stories.* London: Aurum, 2015.

Treadwell, Mattie. *United States Army in World War II: Special Studies; The Women's Army Corps.* Washington, DC: Center of Military History, United States Army, 1991.

Weatherford, Doris. *American Women During World War II: An Encyclopedia.* New York: Routledge, 2010.

Wilcox, Jennifer. *Sharing the Burden: Women in Cryptology During World War II.* Fort Meade, MD: Center for Cryptologic History, National Security Agency, 1998.

———. *Solving the Enigma: History of the Cryptanalytic Bombe.* Fort Meade, MD: Center for Cryptologic History, National Security Agency, 2006.

Williams, Jeannette, with Yolande Dickerson. *The Invisible Cryptologists: African-Americans, WWII to 1956.* Fort Meade, MD: Center for Cryptologic History, National Security Agency, 2001. https://www.nsa.gov/about/cryptologic-heritage/historical-figures-publications/publications/wwii/assets/files/invisible_cryptologists.pdf.

Articles and Pamphlets

Bauer, Craig, and John Ulrich. "The Cryptologic Contributions of Dr. Donald Menzel," *Cryptologia* 30.4: 306–339.

Benario, Janice M. "Top Secret Ultra," *Classical Bulletin* 74.1 (1998): 31–33.

Campbell, D'Ann. "Fighting with the Navy: The WAVES in World War II," in Sweetman, Jack, ed., *New Interpretations in Naval History: Selected Papers from the Tenth Naval History Symposium Held at the United States Naval Academy, 11–13 September 1991.* Annapolis: Naval Institute Press, 1993.

Carpenter, Mary, and Betty Paul Dowse. "The Code Breakers of 1942," *Wellesley* (Winter 2000): 26–30.

Faeder, Marjorie E. "A Wave on Nebraska Avenue," *Naval Intelligence Professionals Quarterly* 8.4 (October 1992): 7–10.

Fairfax, Beatrice. "Does Industry Want Glamour or Brains?" *Long Island Star Journal,* March 19, 1943.

Frahm, Jill. "Advance to the 'Fighting Lines': The Changing Role of Women Telephone Operators in France During the First World War," *Federal History Journal* Issue 8 (2016): 95–108.

Gallagher, Ida Jane Meadows. "The Secret Life of Frances Steen Suddeth Josephson," *The Key* (Fall 1996): 26–30.

Gildersleeve, Virginia C. "We Need Trained Brains," *New York Times Magazine*, March 29, 1942.

Greenbaum, Lucy. "10,000 Women in U.S. Rush to Join New Army Corps," *New York Times*, May 28, 1942, A1.

Guton, Joseph M. "Girl Town: Temporary World War II Housing at Arlington Farms," *Arlington Historical Magazine* 14.3 (2011): 5–13.

Kurtz, Ann White. "An Alumna Remembers," *Wellesley Wegweiser*, Issue 10 (Spring 2003).

————. "From Women at War to Foreign Affairs Scholar," *American Diplomacy: Foreign Service Dispatches and Periodic Reports on U.S. Foreign Policy* (June 2006).

Lee, John A. N., Colin Burke, and Deborah Anderson. "The US Bombes, NCR, Joseph Desch, and 600 WAVES: The First Reunion of the US Naval Computing Machine Laboratory," *IEEE Annals of the History of Computing* (July–September 2000): 1–15.

————. "Secret Keeping 101—Dr. Janice Martin Benario and the Women's College Connection to ULTRA," *Cryptologia* 35.1: 42–46.

Lipartito, Kenneth. "When Women Were Switches: Technology, Work, and Gender in the Telephone Industry, 1890–1920," *American Historical Review* 99.4 (October 1994): 1075–1111.

Lujan, Susan M. "Agnes Meyer Driscoll," *NCA Cryptolog* (August Special 1988): 4–6.

Musser, Frederic O. "Ultra vs Enigma: Goucher's Top Secret Contribution to Victory in Europe in World War II," *Goucher Quarterly* 70.2 (1992): 4–7.

Parker, Harriet F. "In the Waves," *Bryn Mawr Alumnae Bulletin* 23.2 (March 1943).

Rosenfeld, Megan. " 'Government Girls:' World War II's Army of the Potomac," *Washington Post*, May 10, 1999, A1.

Sherman, William H. "How to Make Anything Signify Anything," *Cabinet* Issue 40 (Winter 2010/11). www.cabinetmagazine.org /issues/40/sherman.php.

Smoot, Betsy Rohaly. "An Accidental Cryptologist: The Brief Career of Genevieve Young Hitt," *Cryptologia* 35.2: 164–175.

Wright, William M. "White City to White Elephant: Washington's Union Station Since World War II," *Washington History* 10.2 (Fall/Winter 1998–99): 25–31.

Websites, DVDs, Speeches, Essays

Dayton Code Breakers: http://daytoncodebreakers.org

Undated television interview with Nancy Dobson Titcomb

Fran Steen Suddeth Josephson, *South Carolina's Greatest Generation* DVD, interview with South Carolina ETV, uncut version, undated

Margaret Gilman McKenna videotape interview provided by family

Elizabeth Bigelow Stewart essay of reminiscence

Ann Caracristi speech, "Women in Cryptology," presented at the NSA on April 6, 1998

Larry Gray essay of reminiscence about his mother, Virginia Caroline Wiley, "Nobody Special, She Said"

Nancy Tipton letter of reminiscence, "Memoirs of a Cryptographer 1944–1946," February 2, 2006

Betty Dowse publication of wartime reminiscences by the class of 1942 at Wellesley, "The World of Wellesley '42"

Timothy J. Mucklow essay on the SIGABA Machine, National Security Agency website: https://www.nsa.gov/about/cryptologic -heritage/historical-figures-publications/publications/assets /files/sigaba-ecm-ii/The_SIGABA_ECM_Cipher_Machine_A _Beautiful_Idea3.pdf

President Obama's White House Archives, Fact Sheet on the Normandy Landings, website: https://obamawhitehouse.archives.gov /the-press-office/2014/06/06/fact-sheet-normandy-landings

FURTHER READING

Want to learn more about World War II? Here are some other books on the subject.

Bomb: The Race to Build—and Steal—the World's Most Dangerous Weapon by Steve Sheinkin, published by Roaring Brook Press, 2012. The story of the plotting, the risk-taking, and the genius that went into building the world's most dangerous weapon: the atom bomb.

The Code Book: The Secrets Behind Codebreaking by Simon Singh, published by Delacorte Press, 2002. The incredible true stories of history's most famous code breakers, from Julius Caesar and his infamous Caesar cipher to the Enigma machine the Allies used to decode German messages during World War II.

D-Day: The World War II Invasion That Changed History by Deborah Hopkinson, published by Scholastic Focus, 2018. The World War II invasion known as D-Day was the largest military operation in history. Read about the soldiers, sailors, and paratroopers who made it happen.

Dive! World War II Stories of Sailors & Submarines in the Pacific by Deborah Hopkinson, published by Scholastic Press, 2016. The incredible story of US submarine warfare during World War II.

Eyewitness: World War II by Simon Adams, published by DK Children, 2014. Photographs, illustrations, documents, and maps tell the story of the people, places, and events of the Second World War.

Fly Girls: The Daring American Women Pilots Who Helped Win WWII by P. O'Connell Pearson, published by Simon & Schuster Books for Young Readers, 2018. The story of the remarkable female fighter pilots who answered America's call during World War II.

Lost in the Pacific, 1942 by Tod Olson, published by Scholastic Press, 2016. A true story of survival when a B-17 bomber plane was forced to land at sea.

No Better Friend: Young Readers Edition: A Man, a Dog, and Their Incredible True Story of Friendship and Survival in World War II by Robert Weintraub, published by Little Brown Books for Young Readers, 2016. The story of Frank Williams, a radarman in Britain's Royal Air Force, and Judy, a purebred pointer, who met as prisoners of war during World War II.

INDEX

Page numbers in italics refer to photographs.

Ford, Charles, 97

Forrestal, James, 74

Forrestal, Josephine Ogden, 74

Fort Meade, Maryland, 256

Francis Scott Key Book Shop, 49

French Resistance, 247

"Frequency counts," 29

Friedman, Elizebeth Smith, 17–18, 20–21

Friedman, William F., 17–18, 20–23
  code breaking, 22–24, 26–34, 36–42, 109–10
  code breaking hires, 20, 41, 108, 109
  SIGABA, 236

G

"Garble checks," 65–66

GAT (group as transmitted), 214

Gender roles, 48, 72–73

German Americans, 156, 188

G-girls (government girls), 153

GI Bill, 277–78

Gilman, Margaret, 49, 51, 76, 207

Gliders, 249

Glossary, 299–302

Goucher College, 5–6, 15, 49

Great Depression, 13, 20, 131, 156

Grotjan, Genevieve Marie, 22–23, 35
  code breaking, 22–23, 26, 28, 33–34, 40, 42, 63, 239, 294

Gryphon, 41

Guam, 45, 97, 234

H

Halsey, William "Bull," 111

Harpole, Suzanne, 172, 177

Harvard University, 70, 184

Hazard, Ben, 122–23

"Hello Girls," 212

Hitler, Adolf, 24, 38–39, 63, 237, 243, 257–58
  suicide of, 260, 297

Hogan, Jewel, 105

Hornet, USS, 61

"Hot-bedding," 131, 173–74

Howard, John, 194, 197, 199, 200, 204

Howard University, 106

Hughart, Beatrice, 186, 204, 248–50

Hulick, Veronica Mackey "Ronnie," 185

Hunter College, 87–88, 90, 186

Hurt, John, 20

Hyatt, Betty, 86–87, 97–99

I

Iowa State Teachers College, 85

Italy, 260–61, 296

Iwo Jima, 11, 234, 297

J

Jabberwocky, 41

Jacobs, Randall, 74

JAH, 265, 267

Japan
  declaration of war, 2, 294
  intent to surrender, 264–67
  Pearl Harbor attack, 1–3, 16, 40, 44–45, 170, 294
  surrender, 262, 267–70, 297

Japan Day (V-J Day), 267–69

Japanese Army codes, 108–20, 122–23, 125–30
  2468 (water-transport code), 125–28, 130, 213–19, 228–30, 233–35

Japanese cipher system, 22–24, 26–34. *See also* Purple machine; Red machine

Japanese naval codes, 19–20, 54–57
  JN-20, 69, 178–79
  JN-25, 56–57, 59–60, 64–65, 67–68, 76, 96, 178
  JN-25B, 57

Japanese shipping, 230–34

Jellyfish, 41

Just, Ethel, 106

K

Kamikaze air attacks, 250–52, 264, 280

Kenney, George C., 233

ABOUT THE AUTHOR

Nina Subin

Liza Mundy is a *New York Times* bestselling author and a former longtime reporter for the *Washington Post*. She writes frequently about gender, politics, history, and culture for publications including the *Atlantic* and *Politico*. A senior fellow at New America, she lives in Arlington, Virginia. This is her first book for young readers.

She invites you to visit her at lizamundy.com.